15

minute
parenting
THE TEENAGE YEARS

BOOKS BY JOANNA FORTUNE

JOANNA FORTUNE

15
minute
parenting
THE TEENAGE YEARS

Thread

Published by Thread in 2020

An imprint of Storyfire Ltd.
Carmelite House
50 Victoria Embankment
London EC4Y 0DZ

www.thread-books.com

ISBN: 978-1-80019-093-1
eBook ISBN: 978-1-80019-092-4

The information contained in this book is not advice and the
method may not be suitable for everyone to follow. This book is not
intended to replace the services of trained professionals or to be a
substitute for medical advice. You are advised to consult a doctor on
any matters relating to your child's or your health, and in particular
on any matters that may require diagnosis or medical attention.

For my parents, Tom and Ann Fortune. I am so grateful to have grown up in a playful home; thank you Mam and Dad… PS: teenage me is very sorry ;) X

Joanna Fortune (MICP; MIFPP; Reg Pract APPI; CTTTS; ApSup PTI) is an accredited clinical psychotherapist and attachment specialist. She founded the Solamh Parent Child Relationship Clinic in Dublin in 2010 (www.solamh.com) where she works with families around a variety of issues. She is a recognised supervisor, trainer and conference speaker in her field. In 2017, she delivered a TEDx Talk on the topic 'Social media – the ultimate shame game?' Having previously written a parenting column for *The Sunday Times* (Ireland Edition) she continues to write and contribute to articles on child development and parenting in various other print publications. She is also a regular media contributor to a variety of national radio and TV shows, and the parenting consultant on the weekly parenting slot on Newstalk FM's award-winning *Moncrieff show*. She also hosts her own *15-Minute Parenting* podcast.

CONTENTS

INTRODUCTION

15-Minute Parenting

I am Joanna Fortune, a psychotherapist who specialises in the parent–child relationship from the cradle to the rave, i.e. from pregnancy right up to young adulthood. I have worked in private clinical practice for more than ten years and before this I spent 12 years working in the non-governmental organisation sector in Ireland, including a few years in overseas orphanages. I have worked with hundreds of families across thousands of clinical hours over the span of my career and have progressed to training and supervising other therapists in how to do this specialised work. My 15-Minute Parenting model is the result of all these hours with all kinds of families from a variety of backgrounds in a variety of settings. In my experience, and with very rare exception, most parents are doing the very best that they can and, again with very rare exception, everyone can (re)learn to play and to develop a play-based therapeutic approach to parenting. Across the span of my career and work with families, the most common phrase I hear from parents is that after they've done a day's work, everyone else has arrived back home from school or activities and a dinner is on the table, they feel like ships passing in the night and that they are missing out on those moments of meeting or opportunities for connection with their teenagers. Parents have asked me for ways that they can secure that 15-minute window of connection that they had developed with their younger child now with their teenagers when communication can be more challenging. As before, even 15 minutes of playful and creative communication with your teenagers each day can be good enough to hold and strengthen your connection and, as always, *good enough is good enough.*

Some of us will experience challenges in our parent–child relationship that certainly cannot be addressed or resolved using this model alone and will require the input of a suitably qualified mental-health professional. However, many more of us can experience more mild to moderate-level challenges as our children grow and develop and as our parenting journey grows and develops with them, and this is where my 15-Minute Parenting model is most effective. Even if you are not experiencing challenges in your relationship with your teenager, there is always benefit to be had by increasing and sustaining the level of playfulness in our relationships with our children (regardless of their age), each other and also with ourselves. My model is based on the premise that play isn't a set of activities or games alone but more a state of mind and a way of being. There are benefits in this for all of us in terms of our mental well-being. Always make time and find and create opportunities for play in your relationship with your children, irrespective of their age or stage of development!

In book one of this series I focused on introducing the model, early child development theory and how to apply my model with children aged 0–7 years old. The second book in the series looked more closely at middle childhood, that 8–12-year-old bracket, and this third book will take you through the teenage years. What you will discover in these books is a road map for playful connection and how to learn and use the language of play to strengthen and enhance your relationship with your child throughout your parenting journey.

HOW TO USE THIS BOOK

I have broken the book into themed chapters to cover everything from normal (even when it is unpleasant) adolescent development to the darker side of adolescent behaviour and the brave conversations you will need to engage in with your teenager. The core concept is *creative communication* and I have provided you with lots of therapeutic techniques to add to your 15-minute parenting toolkit that will support you through this stage of parenthood.

I'll show you how you can apply these therapeutic techniques in a playful way that will enable you to better understand your relationship with your children as they grow and develop, and ensure that your parenting is growing and developing with them.

Play continues to serve an important role in teenager's emotional development during adolescence. When they are afforded the opportunity – and indeed encouraged by their parents and important caregivers – to engage in play, young people of this age (13–19 years) show evidence of higher levels of self-esteem, stronger self-efficacy and independence skills, and more resilient mental health.

I am often asked if it is *really* possible to play with our teenagers and my answer is always a resounding yes. Not only is it possible, it is imperative in nurturing the surge in growth and brain development in this stage of childhood. When we worry that our teenagers won't want to play with us, often what we are really worried about is that we don't know how to play with them. We worry that it will feel awkward, and so we avoid it. Well I do this for a living and have yet to meet a teenager who rejects an invitation to play and playfully connect. Depending on the teenager and the stage of the work, I have blown bubbles, thumb wrestled, hand massaged, weather reported, rowed the boat and done clapping games. In fact, most of the play I have previously suggested in this parenting series with younger children I have done with teenagers with only slight modifications.

Throughout this book I am only including the play-based activities that I have used myself with teenagers aged 13–19 years old and that have worked, been well received by this age group and that I know to have brought about a meaningful change to behaviour, emotional expression, open communication and fun connection. I am telling you this not to seek to convince you but more to reassure you that it is possible and essential that we play with our teenagers and that we seek to connect with them in a playful manner. Play remains a language that will fuel connection and nurture your relationship with your teenagers.

WHAT YOU CAN EXPECT TO TAKE AWAY FROM THIS BOOK

This is an age when we are most likely to have stopped playing *with* our teenagers. Often it is parental resistance I meet when suggesting play between parents and teenagers because we struggle to imagine ourselves playing with our teenagers. We feel awkward, so we imagine it will be awkward and we avoid it, telling ourselves that they are too old for play. Well, I have witnessed a marshmallow snowball fight in a home for the elderly with a group of women in their eighties and I can tell you that we are *never* too old for play. Moreover, we *need* play and playfulness in our lives.

This is what I want you to take away from reading this book – that play is not only possible with teenagers, it is vital, it is fun and it is worthwhile!

As you read through this book, I invite you to hold in mind that play is not a box of toys, nor is it even a sequence of activities. Play is a state of mind and a way of being. In order to playfully connect with your teenager, you must be playful within yourself.

This is about grabbing opportunities for shared joy as they arise in your relationship with your teenager.

You will make play possible when you embrace the mantra that *good enough is good enough* and that nurturing your relationship with your teenager is about valuing effort over outcome. Being open to trying something new, to attempt to work it out by yourself is a brave and worthwhile endeavour, even when it doesn't work out as you might have wished it to. I believe that the failings throughout our life serve as a breadcrumb trail of growth and learning and bring us to a place of fresh thinking and new perspective where we shake off the shackles of our *pursuit of perfection* and embrace the authentic learning to be found in *good enough*.

This book is your road map to guide you along the route to relational repair. Just as there is genuine value in trying, failing and learning, there is important learning and an opportunity for growth and development (as a person) in how we negotiate relational rupture (falling out with each other) followed by experiential repair (how we mend that rift and come back together).

These are the core principles of 15-Minute Parenting from infancy and come back into sharp focus now as you prepare to parent through these teenage years. You will row with your teenager. That is a statement of fact and not something to be ashamed of or to avoid. The rows and tension are developmentally unavoidable *but* the key to strengthening and enhancing your relationship with your teenager is *how* you come back together after such a row. This book is filled with practical, playful and creative communication techniques to strengthen and enhance your relationship with your teenagers. Along with gaining a deeper understanding of adolescent (neurological, physical and psychological) development, keeping play alive in your relationship with your teenager will result in *fewer tears and more laughter*.

CHAPTER 1

How to Be Heard Through Those Soundproof Walls of the Parent–Adolescent Relationship

Knowing *what* we want to say and knowing *how* to say it so that it can be heard are very different things. This difference will never be more pronounced than in these teenage years.

Just as there are immense changes to the teenage brain and associated impact for the behaviours and capacity to relate to and connect with others, there are also changes to the various parts of the parenting self that require closer examination and reflection.

If you have read my first book on parenting in the 0–7 years, it is likely some time since you have done so. Or perhaps you are joining me at this stage of parenting and have not seen or done a *parental self-audit* previously. For this reason, I am including it again and encourage you to pause and do this exercise now before you read on.

PARENTAL SELF-AUDIT

Start by asking yourself some questions. The important thing is to answer as fully and honestly as you can, noting if there is something you feel requires further reflection or support to deepen your understanding. For some of us, this further reflection will be a personal contemplative process; for others, we may benefit from meeting with a suitably qualified professional who can support us in working through these blocks. It is important that your reflective process leads to practical actions you can take to address any blocks you might be experiencing. The play and communication techniques detailed throughout this book will help you with this part of your process. Note that this is not in any way intended to be a psychological measure or assessment tool; it is purely for personal and self-reflective use. These questions might include:

- What was growing up like for you?
- In what ways was your relationship with your mother similar to/different from your relationship with your father?
- How were you disciplined as a child and how did this make you feel at the time? How do you feel about it now?
- Who played with you as a child? Do you have memories of your parents playing with and/or singing to you? Can you recall a specific time this happened? What was the game/song? How did it feel when they played with or sang to you? If they didn't, how does that feel to you now, and how might it have felt to you when you were young?
- Did you lose someone important to you through death or moving away? Who was this person and what was their role in your life?
- How were your successes celebrated in your family when you were a child?
- How were your disappointments managed in your family when you were a child?
- Did you have important adults in your life outside your immediate family? Who were they? In what ways were they important to you?
- Did you ever feel unloved or unwanted by your parents? What impact did/does this have on you?

- Do you remember the first time you had to separate from your parents (for at least one day and one night)? How did this feel for you at the time? What was it like when you returned to your parents?
- What would happen when you were sick (so sick you had to stay off school, for example)?
- What would happen when you were hurt (such as falling and cutting your knee)?
- When you think of someone who provided you with comfort and nurture, who comes to mind?
- Did you feel loved as a child? By whom?
- What is your saddest memory from your own early childhood?
- What is your happiest memory from your own childhood?
- When did you realise that you loved your own child? Do you still love them?
- Name three things that you want your child to grow up believing above anything else.

Now write a list of five things that bring you pleasure. These should be things that are about *you*, not about your child or how they might bring you pleasure. Your list might include things like:

- swimming
- running
- football
- golf
- painting/art and crafts
- dinner with friends
- a hot stone massage/blow-dry/facial/nail treatment/haircut/ hot towel/shave, and so on
- a night away alone with your partner.

Now ask yourself when was the last time you got to do each of the things that bring you pleasure. Can you build time into your week to ensure that you do at least one of these things each week? If you can't, ask yourself what needs to change in order for you to be able to do this.

Next, consider how you are currently parenting your child(ren) (if you have more than one child you will have to repeat this for each child – every child is different and how you parent each of them will also be at least slightly different). Ask yourself the following questions:

- Do I find opportunities each day to tell my teen that I love them and that I am proud of them?
- Do I give my teen opportunities to practise independence? Am I developing these opportunities in line with their development?
- Am I able to be firm yet gentle with my teen when necessary?
- Am I safe, predictable, calm and consistent in how I interact with and respond to my teen?
- Do I follow my teen's lead where possible, but take charge when necessary?
- Do I have the opportunity to laugh at least once a day with my teen? Does my teen feel that I enjoy them?
- Do I seek to know the best bit of my teen's day and what bit of their day they would like to change?
- Do I encourage my teen to try new things and to take (appropriate) risks?
- Do I praise their efforts over any outcomes?
- Do I show empathy when my teen seeks my help/support/protection and comes to me for comfort?
- Did I experience repair/recovery following a rupture with my teen today (perhaps not every day)?
- Am I playful with my teen for 15 minutes each day?

- Do I ensure that I affectionately say goodnight to my teen each night no matter what else has/hasn't happened?

A parental self-audit is not a one-time reflection. This is an exercise that you can and should repeat as your child grows up. Deepening our awareness of and insight into our parent-selves is a valuable, ongoing and ever-evolving process. The journey from being a child of a parent to a parent of a child brings up a lot of stuff for all of us. At this stage of parenting, you are also drawing from your lived experience of being the teenager of a parent to being the parent of a teenager. This is why the parent self-audit is worth repeating now, alongside reflecting on each of the parts of our parent-selves.

PARTS OF OUR PARENT-SELF: OUR PARENTAL CORE INSTINCTS

Lean in/Lean out: We have to want closeness and connection in our relationships with our children – truly want it and truly value it in our lives. Intimacy is something that we develop within a trust-based connection that can withstand and survive, and even thrive, within the dance of attachment as it evolves throughout our lives and over the course of our relationships with others. There will be times with everyone in our lives, even our closest and most intimate relationships, when we find it easy to lean in and when we feel the need to lean out and away from them.

Scanning for sense: When we are connected with our children (or others in our lives) we find it easy to scan them and make sense of what they are thinking and feeling. We *mentalise* what another is thinking and feeling and how that makes us think and feel (more on that later in Chapter 6). We do this by assessing and interpreting the other person's non-verbal communication more than their verbal communication. This allows us to *feel* what is happening in the moment with those we feel close to.

Shared joy: In order to sustain something, we have to enjoy it (at least to a degree). This is also true of our relationships and important connections with others. We have to experience pleasure and joy within the relationship to sustain, and in these years, fight for it. This feeling of shared joy is a felt sense of safety and security in the relationship whereby I enjoy you enjoying me, and it gives a child/young person the skills to find and forage joy in their own relationships. It releases dopamine (a happy hormone) in the brain.

Interpretation and translation: We make sense of the behaviour of others *as we experience it*. That is to say, we decide what the meaning and motivation of the other person's behaviour is in terms of how it resonates and makes sense to us. We have to look deeper at what our frame of reference is for this meaning – our own experiences of being a teenager and being parented as a teenager.

Functioning over feeling: To constantly reach out to another and not have them lean in towards you or avail of what you are constantly making available to them is intensely frustrating and disappointing. Repeated and prolonged experience of this emotional rejection of you by your child can contribute to a sense of functional relating over emotional, feeling-based relating. This is a sense of *I will provide you with food and lodgings but beyond that I am done*. Functional care alone does not enable a person to thrive and cannot fuel emotional growth and development. We need those *over and above* care strategies too. The hugs, the smiles, the I love yous, the belief, the desire, the conscious intentions all make a difference. The teenage years will really test this aspect of your parenting.

15-MINUTE EXERCISE

- Bring to mind two words that you would use to describe yourself as a parent.
- Reflect on how these same two words relate to your own parents.
- Do you see them as being connected to how you were parented or are they perhaps a conscious choice to parent in a very different way to how you were parented?
- How does this make you feel now?

Getting *heard* can be a major challenge now, and if this is something that strikes a chord with you, take some time to reflect on *how* you speak as a parent. Do you find that you speak *at* or *with* your child? Do you know how to tell the difference?

HOW TO AVOID A FIX OR CHANGE AGENDA

To strengthen and enhance your emotional connection with your teenager, ensure that you avoid assuming a *fix or change agenda* with them. A meaningful, emotional connection with your child requires a complementary intention; you both have to want a happier and more harmonious relationship with the other. This being said, bear in mind that they are the teenager and you are the adult so you will (more often than not) be driving this connection intention.

Speaking *at* your teenager involves lecturing them. Lectures do not work. Ever. This is because a lecturing approach might initially grab their attention but will not sustain it. Lecture mode evokes defensive responses in your teenager. These might be overt and stated loud and clear (*YOU NEVER LISTEN TO ME*) or involve more non-verbal communications such as eye-rolling, sighing, picking up an object such as a phone, TV remote or magazine to flick through, or physical blocking such as turning away from you or even leaving the room entirely. Lectures are preached and assume a moral authority. They are (mostly) aimed at controlling the young person or exerting a conscious influence over them and this will elicit frustration and potentially shame, which can only reduce their engagement with you and fuel disconnection. They will tune you out. Before you know it, you are ten words into your speech and they have relegated you to white noise. You are now yelling into the wind. It is not landing and you are not 'being heard'.

Similarly, if you default into problem-solving mode, you are pursuing a fix or change agenda. You are moving too quickly towards telling them what they should do to resolve the issue that you have short-circuited (or entirely skipped over) the exploration of emotions and meaning from your teenager's point of view. In my work, I hear so often from teenagers how they just want their parents to listen and hear them in their struggles and not jump in to fix the problem. We do not help our children or young people if we constantly rush to rescue and fix every struggle and problem they have.

What does work is a more narrative, projective 'wondering' approach. This is akin to storytelling. Let them speak and if they are not speaking, 'read and reflect back' their non-verbal communication as you see, interpret and understand it. *I've noticed that you seem out of sorts today. Your shoulders are rounded forward; you're wearing your comfort hoodie and burrowing into the corner of the sofa. I wonder if you'd like a hug from me?* I have not asked my teenager to tell me what's wrong, I have not judged their physical demeanour and demanded that they change it (*Stand up straight, what's wrong with you?*), nor have I judged their emotional demeanour and demanded that they change it (*You're in quite the mood – cheer up for goodness' sake*). What I have sought to do is tell the story of what I am 'hearing' from them. I am communicating that I understand and accept with empathy how they are feeling. I am offering physical comfort in a hug and I do not need them to explain why they need this.

I might want to pursue this further if this overt presentation continues. I will start by telling a story on some neutral but unrelated topic. Perhaps on a theme or about people I know that will interest my teenager.

Storytelling is effective because a story, a well-told narrative, has elements of rhythm (rhythm and synchrony help emotional regulation), suspense (evokes curiosity) and holds attention (fuels engagement). A well-told story relies not only on verbal communication but also non-verbal communication. This means that a parent can use their own non-verbal communication about this story to match and mirror the non-verbal communication they are reading from their teenager. In this embodied way, the teenager will begin to *feel felt* (that is, deeply understood) without having had to share anything overtly with their parent. This will start to bring my teenager in towards me and now I might weave in a more pertinent theme to my story.

I might reflect that I felt low and despondent in hearing/experiencing this first story and I can now choose to tell a story about my own mood or what I think and feel when I am in low or poor form. I want to try to tell this in an authentic manner that doesn't assert that *I know how you feel* but rather seeks to connect over *something in me knows this feeling in you*.

At this stage, you can invite their input. *I wonder what you think? Would you have done this or said something different? What if that was you in this situation? How would you have felt or what might have made you feel better?* Pay attention to their responses and reflections (both verbal and non-verbal). Use the prosody of your voice, which is the musicality and pitch, pace and tone of voice we use to convey meaning when we speak. Now you might wonder how their day was in a casual but enthusiastic and interested (never intrusive) way. You established the connection before you attempted any excavation or correction of their overt behaviour. This is about staying in a position of *not knowing but seeking to better understand* your teenager's felt experience.

This kind of playful yet curious approach helps to generate interest and momentum while attending to emotional security. It reduces the likelihood of defensive avoidance from your teenager and increases the likelihood of true connection that manifests as a moment-of-meeting between you. This storytelling approach allows any discrepancy between what is overtly said and what is not 'said' but embodied to be noticed and even made sense of. When our verbal *and* non-verbal communications match, we will experience a deeper and much more open, fluid style of communication and connection with each other. As humans, we don't just *live* life; we also make sense of it and we achieve this 'sense' by forming coherent narratives that help us to work through and process our experiences. Those of us who can make coherent sense of the experiences we have in our lives are enabled to move forward, unhindered by events of the past. Our aim is always that the experience of 'speaking' about our experiences of events in our lives helps to create an emotional 'felt' safety for our teenagers, and this is best achieved in a secure relationship.

HEALING THE HURTS OF YOUR TEENAGE SELF

It is worth pausing to reflect on your own experience of being a teenager and of being parented as a teenager. If you still have access to your own parents, this can be an interesting social experiment to see how they recall your teenage years and teenage self, versus how you do.

15-MINUTE EXERCISE

- Think of a time when you felt hurt by your parents or by a caregiving adult (teacher/relative).
- How did you respond to this hurt?
- How did your parent/caregiver respond to your hurt?
- Do you think this experience has impacted on how you support your teenager when they speak of feeling hurt by others?

Hurts and rows will happen in the parent–teenager relationship – this is to be expected. It is about what we do after the rupture that will make or break our connection with our teenagers. If you have read the first two books in this series, you will be familiar with me emphasising the importance of rupture being followed (in a timely manner) by relational repair. Repair is always the adult's responsibility. Always. It is vital that we, as parents and important adults in the lives of young people, model good, authentic relational repair. Apologise when things go wrong. The behaviour of the young person should *never* be seen as deserving of more importance and focus than the relationship you have with them. When repair is missed, families run the risk of becoming locked into patterns of avoidance that fuel escalating tensions and conflicts. This resets the temperature of the relationship to constantly simmer and bubble, just waiting for the smallest provocation to erupt. Invest in your relationship with your teenager time and time again and ensure that it is enshrined as something of the highest value because it communicates to your teenager that *they* matter, that you want to stay connected with them and that sometimes you might fight *with* them but you will always fight *for* them. This is why repair is always the responsibility of the parent/adult in charge; it communicates clearly that the relationship is more important than the conflict.

You might pause and reread that last line. It does not only apply to your relationship with your teenager. It can be applied to any and all of your important relationships in your life. Take a moment now to reflect on how you experience and respond to conflict and tension in your life – not just with your teenager but with anyone.

15-MINUTE EXERCISE

- Write down two examples of rupture and repair in everyday life (this can be the small stuff from a throwaway comment over the laundry not being placed in the basket, such as *You're always the same,* to some of the bigger stuff).
- Name three words that describe the emotional impact of rupture (how it leaves you feeling in the moment and immediately afterwards).
- What are the blocks to initiating and accepting repair for you – what stops you reaching out or perhaps accepting the repair (maybe when someone places a cup of tea beside you without words)?
- Name three ways that you 'do' repair – this is not about just saying 'sorry'.
- Think of three actions you make to secure a repair following rupture.

Now pay attention to how easy and how difficult this might have been for you. Acknowledge how easy or difficult you find initiating and/or accepting repair. Acknowledge how rupture in your important relationships leaves you feeling, and become curious now as to where that might have its roots in your life story.

- How was rupture followed by repair in your family growing up?
- Can you think of a specific example of this?
- Did this work well for you? If not, how do you wish your parents had initiated and made repair available to you?

As parents, we are asked to carry out many difficult and emotionally stretching tasks in relation to our children. Our children are 'of us' and, remember, there is no better way to discover your own unresolved issues from your own childhood and being parented as a child than to become a parent. You will start to rediscover this fact now in this stage of your parenting journey as it specifically relates to how you experienced being parented as a teenager. Your own experiences can and will be triggered by some aspect of parenting your teenager now. Pay attention to how you react to your teenager and be honest as to how much of your reaction is about their behaviour or relates more to your own emotionally held experiences being reactivated in these moments.

Be kind and empathic towards yourself and let your teenager see you show yourself kindness. It gives them permission and a road map for how to do this for themselves.

My 15-Minute Parenting model invites and encourages a lot of self-reflection because I know that developing a deeper understanding of our own internal experiences and how these might be impacting on our ability to remain open and engaged with our teenagers is an essential skill in our therapeutic toolkit.

We need to be able to go into our own uncomfortable feelings so that we can take the time to sit with the uncomfortable feelings that our teenagers experience themselves and help them to regulate their arousal levels through calm, clear, consistent co-regulation with you. We can help our teenagers to better understand what is going on for them by developing their own capabilities of reflecting on these difficult and uncomfortable experiences *with* us. They cannot develop this capacity alone.

We must accept that there will be ruptures in our relationship with our teenagers, both because of our need to respond to some of their overt behaviour directly with boundaries and limit-setting or perhaps consequences, and also because of what their words and actions can activate within us that may lead to a rupture in our capacity to emotionally attune to them in the moment. This is healthy and normal in any parent–teenager relationship, and because it is so normal we *must* commit to ensuring that prompt and meaningful repair follows these ruptures. This return to repair is precisely what enables growth and development within our parent–teenager relationship.

You will know that this is working well for you when you can *understand those misunderstandings*; that is, when you can feel calm, comfortable, confident and less anxious when ruptures occur or when uncomfortable issues arise in your relationship.

PLAY TO STRENGTHEN COMMUNICATION WITH YOUR TEENAGER

Human knot: This requires you to have at least five people and is ideal with between seven and ten people. You can invite younger or older members of your family to join in with this one to make up numbers while also encouraging some family play. You stand in a circle and everyone raises their left hand

and reaches out to hold the left hand of someone else (*not* the person either side of you) and then you all do the same with your right hands. Now, without breaking hands, the group must work together to unknot themselves. Success depends on group size, complexity of the knot *but* also communication. Most knots can be solved within 15 minutes but it won't always be possible to work it out, so take it as far as you can in 15 minutes and praise the efforts and good communication skills.

Tip: You could ask one teenager to be your group's director so that they stand apart from the group, moving around to examine and make suggestions to solve it (if you have a larger family or the people around to form a large group), and everyone must follow their direction. Another way of increasing the level of challenge and thereby raising the engagement level is to blindfold some people in the group and only the people without the blindfold can call out solutions and must guide the blindfolded person on their right through the process using clear communication.

Hula-hoop pass: Again standing in a circle of at least five, but ideally more than five, people, hold hands. One person has a hula hoop on each shoulder and begins by dropping them towards the person either side of them. The objective here is to pass the hula hoops around the circle and get them back to the person they started with, without breaking hands. This involves lots of bending, stooping, coordinating and communication between group members. One person will be faced with having to traverse two hula hoops at the same time. Observe how group members help, and encourage them and praise everyone's efforts in this working out.

Tip: Raise the level of challenge by blindfolding every second person so that they must rely on their teammates to work this out.

Obstacle course: You will need at least four people and ideally even numbers, but if you have an uneven number then have the additional member act as observer and sub them in when rotating roles. Players form pairs and one person is blindfolded while the other must successfully guide them around the floor, which is filled with obstacles. These obstacles can be things like cushions and objects but also can be coloured pages that say BOMB/LAVA/FIREPIT and so on. Set a target on the opposite side of the room that everyone should aim for.

Tip: Increase the level of challenge by setting a timer and saying they only have 90 seconds to get across. This one can be played indoors or outdoors. A secondary gain to this one beyond communication is that they must engage in their problem-solving and critical-thinking skills.

It is important to encourage our teenagers to find their voice and to be active and assertive in their own lives *but* it is equally important that we teach them the difference between assertive and aggressive communication.

Fists: You can play this in a pair or have multiple pairs if you want or need to involve more people. Have two pieces of paper with instructions. One of you gets an instruction that reads, *The other person will make a fist with their hand. You must get their fist to open.* The other person will get an instruction that reads, *Make a fist with your hand. The other person is going to try to get it open. You can only open your fist if they assertively and politely ask you to do so.* What typically happens is the first person physically tries to pry their partners fist open using force and the other person responds by using equal force to resist. This is a great game to emphasise the importance of asking for what you want/need rather than just seeking to take or grab it. It also highlights the value of good, clear communication over physical force.

Social situations: For this game you need to prepare three scenarios that require a response from your teenager. You also write *assertive, passive* and *aggressive* on individual slips of paper and put them into a bowl. You will read out each scenario one at a time and your teenager must pick a communication style out of the bowl and respond in this way. You can guess the style they are using. It is good to reflect afterwards how it felt and what style they felt most comfortable using and what style might be most effective. Your scenarios can be anything but should be relatable to your teenager's life. Here are some ideas:

- Your teacher has kept you back after class to tell you off for only turning in half of the assignment.
- Your friend is 45 minutes late meeting you and now you have missed the start of the movie.
- You are returning an item of clothing but you don't have a receipt so the sales assistant is refusing a refund.
- Your elderly neighbour spots you on your way out and calls you over to complain to you about playing music loudly in the evening time.
- Your friends all think that you did something you didn't do. You know the main person saying it was you is actually the one who did it.

I also find these communication activities playful but fun to do with teenagers of any age:

Messenger: You will need three or more people. One person acts as the runner and two are builders, identified as A and B (if you have more people, they are observers and get to step in and have a go when this round is done). The two builders are each given a set of identical building blocks and stand away from each other, with their backs turned so they cannot see what the other is doing. Person A builds a structure. The runner watches them do this and goes back over to person B and tells them how to build the structure based on what they have observed. At the end, the aim is that both structures will be identical based on the good communication of the runner.

Sit-down game: This is another fun game that reinforces the skill of reading non-verbal communication. There are two ways to do this and it works best if you have a family or group of four or more people. Set a rule that two people must be standing at any one time but *only* two people. These two people can only stand for 20 seconds at a time. So if Mum and eldest child are standing, within 20 seconds (any time within this, as it cannot pass 20 seconds) they must sit down (not at same time necessarily), and as they move to do so, the others must anticipate their action and stand up before they sit, so that two people are always standing. Another way to do this is to have everyone stand in a circle and nominate a leader for each round. The group stands in silence and watches for when the leader moves to sit, as the whole group must sit down at the exact same time. If anyone is out of sync, they all get back up and wait and try again.

Describe and draw: This is a fun game to play that supports communication too. Take two chairs and place them so that two people are seated back to back. One is identified as A and the other as B. A is handed an object by another person (if you have them) or simply picks an object themselves and must verbally describe that object without naming what it is. B must draw the object based on A's description and see if the object can be matched/identified at the end.

Play is a great and very effective interactive way to support your child's evolving communication skills. It is also a good way to strengthen and enhance your own communication with your teenagers in a way that is positive, fun and laughter based.

Non-verbal communication is another great skill to build on through play and is also a great way to connect when your teenager is barely speaking to you. Also, eye contact is one of the basic principles of communication and trusting others.

Eye-contact circle: Create a circle with the entire family or whoever is available for your group. The aim here is to secure eye contact with someone else in the circle and once you do, the person you are looking at must answer the group's pre-agreed question, which might be something like, 'What is your favourite snack or flavour of ice cream/breakfast cereal? After answering the question, they must then find mutual eye contact with someone across the circle who then answers the question, and so on.

Swapsies: In this version, once eye contact is made, the people must silently switch places with them, while maintaining that eye contact. For round two, once eye contact is made, meet in the middle and add in a non-verbal greeting such as a high five, handshake, wave, elbow bump, toe tap.

For round three, once eye contact is made and they meet in middle with their non-verbal greeting, they add in a verbal greeting, such as 'Hi', 'How are you?' or 'Hello'.

CHAPTER 2

Adolescent Development

There are lots of scary stories in the media about what can and sometimes does go wrong in adolescence, but it is important to remember that adolescence is a natural developmental stage for both you and your child to go through. This is about informing yourself, preparing yourself, accepting the inevitability of change in your child and your relationship with them and (as best you can) keeping the lines of communication open while you both adjust.

A teenager might be defined as someone aged between 13 and 19 years old, but the definition of adolescence is that period following the onset of puberty during which a teenager develops from a child into an adult. This journey from childhood into adulthood is a monumental developmental leap and naturally is not without its trials and tribulations (for both parent and teen) along the way.

It is often said that the early years are the most demanding years in parenting, but I do not share this view. I believe that adolescence is the most demanding time of parenting and, moreover, that adolescence is a second bite at the developmental apple. This means that what went well in those early years will now require topping up and even some fine-tuning (remember that small changes make big differences in parenting) but even if (or perhaps especially if) those early years were not so successful, you now have an opportunity to repeat those developmental steps in adolescence. This is not to say that you parent your teenager as though they were a toddler *but* the focus in those early years is on boundaries and limit-setting, opportunities for independence and using your own social engagement system[1] to stimulate, engage and co-regulate your child's developing social engagement system. In essence our SES picks up signals from others, such as body language, voice quality and facial expressions, and interprets what it picks up and cues us to react/respond/reflect. If the SES likes what it sees and hears, we experience calm, and if not we experience fear. This is an unconscious process so we do not have overt control over it or how it operates.

Now that you are faced with a teenager, whose physiological and psychological development is on fire, these same parenting goals apply, but you must *grow up* your parenting to reach them.

When children are very young, they are in love with their parents. They idealise their parents and see that their parents know all the answers and can fix everything. This begins to wane a bit in middle childhood, though you remain the reliable soundboard for the big stuff. Now that your child is a teenager they will present as intensely disappointed in you, sigh in exasperation at how little you know and rather than seeing you as someone with the solutions to problems, you *are* the problem. But the teenage years are not all doom and gloom. This is also a time of great excitement and change as you see your small child blossom and grow into a young adult. They have their own beliefs, passions, causes and outlooks and are more than prepared to fight you on those.

This is a time of great neurological, physiological and psychological development and these can be broken down into three stages of adolescence and the all-important five adjustments of adolescence.

THREE STAGES OF ADOLESCENCE

Early adolescence (12–14 years)

This is peak puberty time and teens begin to spend longer periods of time scrutinising their appearance. With this increased self-focus can come raised levels of embarrassment (blushing, apparent shyness) and while they are more focused on their physical appearance, they react badly if you show too much interest in it. You will likely see a noticeable increase in risk-taking behaviour and ultimately pushing of boundaries. Communication shifts more towards what is *not said* than what is *said*. Early adolescents display very black-and-white thinking and can be quite fixed and rigid in their thinking, meaning that they can become overtly argumentative and can struggle to keep in mind that there can be an opposing view/belief to their own without an opposing view being a direct challenge to or attack on them. This is largely because teenagers are still evolving in their capacity to mentalise – that is, to understand how they think and feel about something while also understanding how someone else is thinking and feeling about the same thing. This is also described as being able to keep a mind in mind and understand that we make inferences about situations, scenarios and people and that inferences, by their nature, are prone to errors so that we might be right and we might be wrong about them. This is exactly what allows us to understand that different people can see and understand things in different ways. Healthy mentalisation is one of the best mechanisms we have to safeguard and strengthen our mental health and emotional well-being so I will discuss it in more detail in Chapter 6.

Sexual interest is becoming piqued, and you will notice intense crushes and fantasies about celebrities and musicians. This is also a time when sexual identity issues come into sharper focus and you may see more overt questioning about their sexual identity. This is entirely normal and healthy, and I will discuss sexual identity issues in Chapter 7. Starting in middle childhood and now increasing in these adolescent years, their peer group becomes a more important hub of social development than their immediate family. Parents are no longer idealised; indeed your early adolescent will have no issue in pointing out all of your limitations and failings to you at this stage. This shift brings new acting-out types of behaviours with it. Puberty is amplified at this stage (especially for girls as they tend to enter puberty earlier than their male counterparts), and mood swings can be quite extreme, oscillating between rage and apparent depressed states.

Mid-adolescence (15–17 years)

The surge of puberty has settled (at least for girls, whereas boys may be still in the midst of puberty at the start of this stage, with changes to their voice and physical appearance ongoing) but mood swings will linger. The heightened focus on appearance is still there, and now they are not only focused on how they look but also on how they are convinced others are perceiving – and moreover judging – how they look. Their withdrawal from their parents increases because they perceive that you *just don't get it* and are convinced that you are out to *ruin* their life. They crave increased independence, but how they assert this can be very confusing for parents, who often respond by increasing control and structure in the belief that their teen is not mature enough to have this level of independence. For example, they might assert their independence with poor hygiene because they believe it is up to them when they shower, or they may refuse to tidy their bedrooms in the belief that it is *their space* to structure as they see fit and you shouldn't have a say in that. You, as their parent, may see their seeming inability to shower and maintain a clean sleeping space as evidence of their immaturity and as such respond by increasing your control by decreeing when they should shower and threats about consequences for the messy or even dirty bedroom. This stand-off will lead to increased tensions and rows.

Their peer group is their main focus and their position within that group is what drives their behaviours and actions. You will see an increase in risk-taking behaviour (more on that later), but you will start to see a decrease in those acting-out behaviours that are so marked in early adolescence as their ability to better verbalise what is going on has increased. This doesn't mean you won't still see those acting-out behaviours – you most certainly will, but not as frequent as in early adolescence and the voracity of such behaviours will have decreased.

Note: I want to emphasise that this is a very general developmental overview and I am very aware that some teenagers will display extreme behaviours throughout their adolescence. We see other contributing variables at play (life events, mental illness, traumatic experiences) when earlier developmental behaviours linger into mid- and even later adolescence. If this describes your relationship with your teenager, see Chapter 8.

Brain development continues throughout adolescence, and as a result, teenagers and young adults do not think, perceive, process or reflect in the same way that adults do. Keeping this in mind and increasing your awareness of adolescent brain development and the associated behaviours this development brings will be immensely supportive to you as you grow your parenting up in line with your adolescent's development. This understanding helps to reassure you that you are not living with an alien/sociopath, so I will be discussing adolescent brain development later on.

Late adolescence (18–21 years)

By now, most adolescents have completed physical growth and we tend to see a balance between risk and reward, and an ability to consider likely consequences of certain actions, bringing better impulse control with it. While they tend to have secured greater independence and even (literal but certainly figurative) distance from their parents, they will also be re-establishing a more adult connection and relationship with them. In this stage, parents become more 'peer' than 'adult-in-charge' and they will discuss more mature and world/current-affairs topics with you. They will have a clear stance and position on such matters and are strengthening their individuality, values and ideals. There is a greater degree of stability in their relationships (friends, intimate partners and family).

The job of parenting is to raise independent adults. So what if your late adolescent refuses to move on… and move out? Failure to launch is a growing issue in a world plagued with housing crises and with young adults spending longer in full-time education than previous generations. They also tend to change jobs and even careers with quicker frequency than previous generations, so are less financially secure and therefore less able to live independently. But more than this, I think there is a strong psychosocial aspect to failure to launch and will discuss this in Chapter 9.

FIVE ADJUSTMENTS OF ADOLESCENCE

While there are three stages of adolescence, there are five key developmental adjustments and these apply to both teenagers *and* parents. These adjustments are often unpleasant to parent through but they are not to be pathologised. They might be challenging, but they are not a developmental problem per se. This is important as often it is something in this range of developmental adjustment that brings a parent to consult with me or to seek to refer their adolescent to see me. This can be a tricky set of adjustments and you need creative ways to parent through the challenges they bring.

1. Ignorance

Your teenager is becoming more private and secretive, and when a parent knows less, they tend to worry much more. How you handle this worry is what makes or breaks this adjustment in adolescence.

Lisa's story (15 years old)

Fifteen-year-old Lisa stormed into my consulting room and flung herself onto the couch. Her face glowered and through gritted teeth she growled, 'That nosy cow.'

I sat back and paused before saying, 'Lisa, you… are… FURIOUS today.'

'I know that she's been reading my journal. She keeps bringing up things that I've written about as though they just occurred to her and giving me all the ways she *would handle it. She is so transparent!'*

I interjected to acknowledge what I had heard, and empathised that this must have felt very uncomfortable for her even if her mother had seen herself as being helpful.

'That's exactly what she *said when I caught her out. Even though I knew she was reading my journal, I wanted to have evidence so that she couldn't deny it so I wrote a fake entry about being worried that I might be pregnant and sure enough she lost it and tried to force me to take a pregnancy*

test in front of her. I asked her why she thought I might be pregnant and she had to admit to reading my journal. When I told her I had planted that entry, she had the nerve to get angry with me, saying I was sly and had set her up. She's the one in the wrong and she needs to apologise to me!'

Lisa's mother acted out of genuine concern, but her method of doing so was intrusive rather than being interested in her daughter's life. They needed support in finding that line between Lisa needing increased privacy and her mother needing to know what was going on. The trust in the relationship was still fractured after a very difficult early adolescence stage for Lisa. Lisa felt she had made all kinds of changes in her behaviour (accurate to be fair to her) and her mother felt that Lisa still couldn't be trusted (there had been significant risk-taking behaviour 12–18 months before this).

Her mother joined us for some joint sessions so that we could work directly on the rupture in trust and clarify that while Lisa's mother needed to work on her demand to know everything that was going on in Lisa's life, Lisa had to develop a better understanding of how privacy could be retained with more transparent communication. They agreed to have a 'café chat' each week for one hour, where they would sit in a café for a drink and a phone-free chat about the highs and lows of each of their weeks, with neither being under pressure to share more than they felt comfortable with. We role-played this in session to prepare both for the exercise. Initially we had to structure this time, but as they moved forward it became more fluid and natural.

15-MINUTE SOLUTION: CAFÉ CHAT

Agree a set time each week that you will go to a café and sit together to talk about the highs and lows of your week. To ensure your teen doesn't simply sit back and allow *you* to fill the hour, structure it further with each of you speaking for 15 minutes at a time. This should be entirely uninterrupted, and by assigning 15 minutes it means that neither of you can just name two brief facts but must provide some more detail by telling the story of that high or low. When one has finished talking (if it goes on longer than 15 minutes allow that, as the structure is flexible not rigid remember), the other has up to 15 minutes to respond and reflect what they have heard, ideally with empathy and acceptance and avoiding judgement and giving advice (this might take practice initially). Then the roles switch and the other person gets to talk about their highs and lows for 15 minutes before the other one responds in the same way. Through repeated experience, both parties can learn how to communicate in a more connected way and stay in an *interested* rather than *intrusive* mode.

2. Estrangement

Your teenager is now differentiating themselves from how they were as a child. You will also observe significant changes in terms of how they now see and experience who you are to them. They experiment with new tastes/styles/interests/friendships as a means of asserting this difference; parental connection becomes more difficult as you feel your teenager pull away from you and set their identity as 'other' than you.

Craig's story (16 years old)

Sixteen-year-old Craig arrived in my office dressed in black with multiple piercings and a Mohawk hairstyle with lots of colours on the tips of each spike. I wondered how long it took to do his hair each day and he said, 'Not long now that I'm used to it. Why, do you think it looks bad too?' I reflected that some people had an issue with his hair and wondered if he would like to talk a bit about that.

'Oh not just my hair – my piercings, my clothes and of course the tattoo… I mean, you know this – you've met my parents, haven't you?'

I took this to be Craig's way of wondering what preconceived ideas I might have about him as a result of having met his parents first. I acknowledged that his parents struggled with the changes he had made to his style and that I was more curious as to what he made of this.

'This goes way back. When I was fourteen years old I started dyeing my hair and got some new piercings. I knew then it bothered them, but I liked it and they don't get to tell me who I am. That should be up to me, so I've added more piercings and changed hair colour a few times now. I like how I look, and I like changing how I look.'

I reflected that it was important to be happy with how you look and that it can be fun to experiment with styles and tastes. I added, 'It also makes you look really different from anyone else in your family I'm guessing.' I wondered why he thought his parents had an issue with his style. His parents had come to me off the back of a new tattoo he'd had done. His parents had said that they didn't approve of his style and image because they feared that it would attract negative attention and make him vulnerable to attack.

'It's about control for them, I think. They say things like "The state of you" and "Do you know or even care what people will think when they see you?", "You're making yourself a target", "This is all attention-seeking, Craig. Why are you so desperate for attention?" I get a lot of "You cannot go out like that".'

So while his parents felt worry, he heard control and judgement. I asked him to tell me the story of his tattoo, as that is what had prompted this referral.

'I love art. I spent months researching the design for this tattoo. I actually drew and designed it myself and met with the tattoo artist a couple of times to talk about how it would work as a tattoo and made changes accordingly. It took a few appointments to get it done and I paid for it all myself with money I had saved from my birthday and Christmas. I really love it, but they act like it was a whim and that I'll regret it.'

I focused on the fact that it was his own design and remarked on how talented he was. I didn't get into whether he was right or wrong about the tattoo because I wanted to follow the thread of his passion and what he identified with. He became more animated than he had been so far in our session as he spoke about art, methods and genres. The following week he brought me his sketchpad and showed me more of his work. He said that the tattoo studio had commissioned three designs from him for clients who had admired the photo they had of his tattoo. I said, 'It's really nice to have your talent acknowledged, isn't it?'

Over the following weeks, Craig shared some deeper-held thoughts and beliefs he had about art and skin as canvas and the body holding and telling a narrative. His tattoo, just like his hair, piercings and clothing, was not whimsical; nor was it a rebellious acting-out as his parents had long since believed (hence their fear that the permanence of a tattoo would be *something he would regret when this phase passed). This was very much Craig exploring and expressing his identity in a way that was personal, considered and important to him.*

He agreed to his parents joining us for some dyadic (joint) sessions so that we could bring both narratives together. My role was to hold a shared space and support Craig to find the words to tell the story of his identity to his parents and show that beneath the exterior of tattoos and piercings was still their smart, sensitive, caring and very talented son. His parents were able to rediscover who lay beneath the surface that had seemed so strange and unrelatable to them. A stronger acceptance and increased tolerance from both sides emerged.

On our last joint session, Craig arrived with a gift bag and he presented it to his parents with a framed drawing he had done. They were overwhelmed by his gesture and one said, 'Gosh, we have an original piece by Craig. This will be worth a fortune one day,' while the other added, 'It's priceless already.'

15-MINUTE ART ACTIVITY

This is an activity I did with Craig and his parents and one that I think is worth trying at home with your teenager certainly, but perhaps the whole family can work on this together. Pick a theme. I chose **words to live by**. I asked them to spend the time before the next session gathering newspaper and magazine cuttings or words, phrases and images that encapsulated the words they each chose to live by. I asked that they did this individually and did not share what they had gathered until we all met together. When they arrived, I had a poster board and some glue set up and invited them to each choose ten words/phrases/images from their selection and then share what they had chosen with each other. What jumped out was how in sync they were with their values as so many of their words, phrases and images aligned with each other's. This was a moment of clarity for Craig's parents and as they compiled their collage it reminded all of them that they were still more alike than not.

You will need:

- old magazines, newspapers, picture books and scrap paper
- coloured pens and pencils
- scissors and glue
- cardboard or thick paper for the base of the collage.

Begin by:

1. Ask everyone to take a moment to reflect on their core values. For younger children in your family or even for some teenagers, you may want to discuss what you mean by values by asking them what sort of things they feel strongly about, or what they feel good about when they see how other people behave and how they behave.
2. Start by saying you will each close your eyes, take three breaths and see what words, colours, shapes, phrases and images immediately pop into your mind.
3. Once ready, everyone should begin selecting images, words, phrases or colours from the magazines and newspapers. You can either work all together or on separate collages. I prefer this to be a shared/joined activity and suggest you

use a large poster board and even assign sections to each person to work on separately, but the end result should be a shared collage.

4.   If they feel comfortable, save some time at the end of the activity for everyone to present their contribution to the family collage and share what it means to them.

---

3. Abandonment

This is about the adolescent desiring increased separation from their parents, along with more independent social interaction. This means that they have less time for their parents, which means their parents may miss them and feel that they have to compete for their teen's time and attention.

Kate's story (13 years old)

Thirteen-year-old Kate sat curled up in the corner of the couch in my clinic room. She was softly spoken and mostly looked down at her lap. She spoke about school and friends and how many siblings she had and when I asked how she got on with her parents, she started to softly cry. I reflected, 'It's difficult for you to think about that relationship, Kate. I wonder why.'

'I'm not a good person anymore. I have such awful thoughts about them when they do so much for me. There's something badly wrong with me – there must be. My mum and I used to be so close and we did so much together. I loved spending time with her and now I cringe at the idea of having to be seen with her. I don't know what's changed. My mum is the same as she always was. She still buys me things she sees

in shops, but I just hide them in the back of my wardrobe or say they didn't fit when she asks about them. She suggests we go to the movies like we always did, but I just don't want to spend that much time alone with her. I'm a terrible person.'

I asked what she did like to spend her time doing now.

'I just want to hang out with my friends from school or spend time in my room on my phone chatting with friends. It's this Friday night thing that's causing the most trouble. You see, my group of friends all spend Fridays in each other's houses after school. We take turns with whose house it's to be and we order pizza and hang out and sometimes sleep over in the person's house; well, most of the time we sleep over. It's usually a late night and I'm kind of tired on Saturdays. My mum and I always went swimming on Saturday mornings and then we would go shopping in the town centre and have some lunch together. It was kind of "our thing" 'cos, you know, I'm the only girl at home and she doesn't do that with my brothers. But now I want to be able to come home and get some sleep on Saturday mornings and then meet my friends to go shopping in the afternoon. I feel badly about pushing my mum away when she keeps suggesting stuff with me, but why won't she just take the hint and stop asking me when it's obvious I have other plans and just can't go with her?'

Kate presented a classic example of this adjustment in adolescence. She could reflect on what her relationship with her mum was and she was reaching for that social independence but being an emotionally sensitive teen she could see that her mum was struggling and felt badly that she was abandoning her. But this adjustment is dependent on some degree of abandonment and Kate needed to surge forward with her development. Together we wondered about how this push/pull sense of desire versus duty was for Kate and how it might be for her mum. I wondered what Kate would advise *her friend to do in the same situation and had her role-play that scenario with me. A few weeks later, she came in smiling and said that she had talked with her mum about changing their weekly time together and now they were going to the cinema and for some food on a Wednesday afternoon instead. She was pleased that she had resolved the issue, then added, 'Of course, not every Wednesday because sometimes I have things on after school, but definitely one Wednesday a month.'*

The need to pull away and prioritise the relationships outside home is a very normal and healthy development in adolescence. That being said, it can be very difficult for both teenager and parent to negotiate this apparent abandonment and find a new way of connecting within this increased distance. It can feel like a huge loss for a parent who longs for that closeness again with their child, but it is also very important that a parent can contain those feelings and not make them the responsibility of their teenager.

Tips to help you to manage this separation and all it brings up

Invest in yourself at this time. Ensure that you have something and someone in your life, outside the immediate family, whom you meet up, connect, unwind and laugh with. Perhaps join a book club, hold a monthly dinner with friends, take up an old interest again or even a new one, join an exercise class or something sensory and creative, such as an art class. I did this myself in the last year and trust me, you do not have to be particularly artistic or talented (I am certainly not) to draw benefit from it. It is about creating time that is yours and about you – not about you as a parent/professional/spouse, but simply about and for you as a person. Having your own interests like this can be really helpful to offset some of these feelings of loss.

Alongside this though, it can be nice to find creative ways to reconnect when your teenager is at home and 'with' you. Playing with nurture is a nice way to achieve this.

Invite your teenager to lie down on the sofa and rest their head on your lap. Tell them to close their eyes while you give them a **cotton-ball face massage.** This is a great way of communicating in a doing not saying way that you get that they've had a bad day, or are feeling low, or have fallen out with their friend, or just need a bit of extra minding. There is no demand that they tell you what has happened, but there is connection and a moment of meeting between you both.

Using a cotton ball, apply enough pressure that they really feel it – not so much that it hurts or is uncomfortable pressure and not so little that it feels tickly and irritating on the skin. The right amount of pressure triggers that proprioceptive effect whereby your touch cues the skin to send a message of reassurance to the brain. It calms, soothes and reassures. Trace the cotton ball all around their face – over their forehead, around their cheek, under their chin and up and around the other cheek. Bring it down the bridge of their nose and up and down the sides before tracing over eyebrows and then very lightly over eyelids, as this is a more sensitive spot. Repeat this for as long as feels comfortable for them. They might even fall asleep while lying there. It sounds simple, but in part that is precisely why this one is really effective.

4. Control

This is about the teenager leaving the age of command (parents must be obeyed) and entering the age of consent (belief that compliance is now up to them) by using active resistance (argument) and passive resistance (delay). Parents may become more frustrated at powerlessness but you must continue to assert your influence.

Sophie's story (14 years old)

Fourteen-year-old Sophie came to see me with what her parents described as increasingly challenging behaviour. She had been in trouble at school as well as at home and they said that she just didn't seem to care. They believed she had problems with authority, and home life had become a war zone.

'My dad is a TOTAL CONTROL FREAK but I showed him that he won't control ME! My dad has always seen himself as the boss in our family and it has always been easier to just go along with him than fight it, but I've had enough and just decided no more.'

It is worth noting that while her dad was indeed a stickler for rules, most of what he insisted on was actually quite reasonable stuff (everyone eat together at the table, the need to be punctual so that everyone could leave the house on time in the morning, not slamming doors, etc.). However, his rigidity and inflexibility about those rules being adhered to at all times and issuing quite radical consequences (he had thrown all of her make-up out when she was consistently late leaving the house on the basis of 'one less thing to do in the morning') was a significant trigger for her own behaviour.

'I know that if I want to set him off, all I have to do is slam my bedroom door – it drives him mad. So when he wouldn't let me go to a party with my friends I got so angry that I just slammed my door in his face. I wanted him to just stop talking at me and leave me alone, but I also knew it would make him angry, just like I was angry. But this time there was just silence after the door slammed. And then he came back with a screwdriver and took my door off the hinges and carried it away. I mean, WHO DOES THAT? Then he said that I would have to earn my door back – well, I knew how to "earn" it back alright. I just went about my personal

routine, you know getting undressed, shaving my legs, air-drying after my shower and all of that stuff, but because I had no door he didn't want to walk past my room in case I was doing something private… eh, that is the literal point of having a door, right? So, after a couple of days I came home from school to find my door was back on its hinges. I guess I won that round and showed him!'

I'm not saying Sophie was right here but the crux of the challenges at home and indeed at school was that Sophie did not believe she needed to 'do as she was told anymore'. A strict and disciplinarian parent had raised her, and this resistance to command was a rebellion against all of that. I did some psycho-educational work with her parents around adolescent development and about structure and boundaries (gentle yet firm, while flexible and adaptable to circumstances) rather than rigid rules. We worked on ways to connect with Sophie rather than their interactions always being based on behavioural correction. Sophie and I continued to work together around the other issues for a few months after this, but this shift in parental behaviour was immensely helpful in being able to get behind her rebellious exterior.

This is clearly an example of active resistance, but passive resistance can also be a major hotbed for tensions at home between parents and children. You know it well. This is where you ask your teenager to take the rubbish out to the bin and they respond with an almost reassuring, 'Yeah, I'll do it in a minute.' But they don't, do they, and when you repeat yourself, maybe a little more urgent in tone, they again say 'I'll do it in a minute.' After an hour passes you are huffing and muttering as you stomp past them, taking the rubbish out to the bin yourself. And as you berate them for never helping you out or doing what you ask of them, they glance up from their phone to say, 'What's your problem? I said I would do it in a minute.' And now you are in a command struggle, just as above with Sophie.

15 minutes of collaboration a day

Sophie and her dad benefitted from increasing the time they spent together collaborating on a project. In reality, they spent more than 15 minutes a day working on this, but the point here is to take something that you can gradually work on over a period of time, doing a small amount every day. Sophie wanted a desk space in her room where she could do her homework. Her dad brought home a really old school-style classroom desk (one that had space for an inkwell) and suggested they upcycle it together. We had agreed in advance that he would take the support role in this activity and that the colour and design would be entirely up to Sophie. They worked together each day to clean, then sand and then paint and polish it.

5. Conflict

This is where a teenager will be more abrasive in the process of opposition, which is aimed at liberating themselves from parental rules and requirements so that they can claim independence. This frequently leads to increased rows with parents who see that their child has become more pushy and less pleasing to live with.

David's story (17 years old)

Seventeen-year-old David had been a calm and level-headed 'good kid' throughout his adolescence. But at 17 years old he had started a serious relationship and his parents said that this was when the difficulties began.

'I'm not the one who needs to be in therapy, my parents are! I'm practically an adult; they have to step back and respect me. Once I turn 18 and finish school, they can't interfere in my life anymore anyway.'

I wondered what being legally an adult would mean for him.

'It's about choice, isn't it? Being able to make my own choices without having those choices judged and criticised. My parents don't drink alcohol or believe in sex before marriage. They're really religious, which is fine, but what's not fine anymore is that they expect, actually demand, that I live my life according to their beliefs and rules. I mean, it's not like I'm coming home drunk or getting into trouble when I am out; I'm not and I know that loads of teenagers do. Of course, having a perfect older sister isn't helpful here because any small thing I do that they don't agree with seems so much worse because she never breaks any of their rules. The real issue here is that they don't like my girlfriend. They think it's because of her that I'm doing things that they don't agree with, which is insulting to me and to her.'

He lit up as he described an exciting, vivacious, spirited young woman who held liberal beliefs and was an active campaigner on many social causes. He said that he met her at a youth forum for civic participation between a number of schools in his area and that he couldn't take his eyes off her. She was passionate and spirited and very much 'her own person'. She encouraged him to also be his own person. He had started to stay over with her at her house, though he had told his parents he was at a friend's house. He was aware that they knew he was lying, but neither they nor he had called that out. They found alcohol in his wardrobe that he had bought to take to a party and this is what prompted the referral to me. He had packed his bag, taken his beer and stayed away from home for the weekend with friends. I wondered how his parents experienced this.

'They went mad. They were so angry, and then my mother cried and that kind of broke my heart because I hadn't meant to upset her; I just want to be able to make choices on my own and do normal stuff. Why can't they accept that I'm just not like them and let me live my life my way?'

This theme of living his life and becoming his own person was very pronounced in my work with David. As time went by, a narrative emerged that he really hadn't negotiated many of the adjustments of adolescence and just went along with how things were. He said that he had written lyrics instead of arguing or fighting back with his parents – he had dozens of notebooks filled with lyrics. I invited him to read from some of these and we worked around what themes and memories these readings brought up for him.

'I know that turning 18 isn't going to just magically change things at home because, as they keep reminding me, it's their house and their rules and I do actually understand that. That's why I made the decision to change my college application form to only apply to colleges that would require me to live away from home. I think it's the best solution for all of us.'

It's not for me to say if the actions taken by either teenager or parent in any of these scenarios are right or wrong. I am focused on what works or doesn't work within a parent–teenager relationship and how to support both parties to find their own narrative while empathising with each of their narratives. David's solution might not be the ideal one, but it gave him access to space to further explore himself, even if the ongoing conflict was not addressed head-on.

Years later his mother contacted me regarding something else and she said, 'David lives a different life to the one we lead, but he's grown into a fine young man and we're so proud of him and all he's achieved.' She said that their relationship was on good terms and they spent plenty of time together as a family, and she frequently met him for dinner where he lives and works. He had never lived at home full-time since leaving school.

You will have seen that teenagers present with a variety of challenges around each of these adjustments, and remember that while I have given you an example of a teenager's struggle with just one adjustment, the reality is that all teenagers go through each of these so you might recognise elements of each story in your one teenager. You will also see that in each story the teenager in question felt vehemently that they were in the right and that their parent just didn't 'get it' or get them. This is a period of emotional disconnect in terms of teenagers tuning you out and minimising what you say as being simply not clued in with how their world works. You will feel as if you are trying to communicate through an impenetrable wall. The only outcome of this stand-off is increasing frustration for all involved.

FIVE PARENTAL ADJUSTMENTS NEEDED IN ADOLESCENCE

These adjustments are difficult and challenging without a doubt, but as a parent you will have more difficulty during these adjustments if you refuse to let go of the parent–child relationship so that the parent–adolescent one can emerge!

Parents often express their own difficulty in adjusting during this phase through statements they make.

About ignorance: 'I must know everything that is going on'

Pam's story (parent)

Pam contacted me with concerns about her teenage daughter. She felt that she was shutting down, becoming very secretive and withholding things from her. Before I could say anything she said, 'Now I know you'll say that all teenagers do this, but this is not my teenager. We're so close and she tells me everything – she always has. Something is wrong here.'

I suggested that she came in to see me alone without her daughter. She arrived and very quickly took a second phone out of her handbag and without missing a beat she said, 'This is my daughter's phone. She doesn't know I have it – she would go mad actually – but she's not allowed it in school so she leaves it in my car so she can have it on the way to and from school.'

I put up my hand and said, 'Pam, I'm going to ask that you put your daughter's phone back in your bag. We will not be reading her messages in here.'

Pam was initially indignant and defensive, asking how else could she know what was happening in her daughter's life if she didn't look through her phone. I suggested that we start at this point: how it felt to be pushed to the outside of her daughter's life and to know so little about what was going on. Pam cried immediately.

She cried for some time, and when she stopped, she said, 'We were so close; I thought we always would be.'

This was not an issue of trust, but it was one of boundaries. Pam trusted her daughter; she just missed her. She missed being her confidante and her friend. She missed being the one her daughter brought everything to and whose opinion she always sought and valued.

'She had her hair cut last weekend – as in completely restyled. It's lovely but she didn't even tell me she was doing it; she didn't even show me the style she was thinking of to ask my opinion.'

We worked together using psycho-education and therapeutic parenting to support Pam to process her feelings of loss and get back to a place where she could establish a new stage of her relationship with her daughter.

15-MINUTE SOLUTION

Movie magic: This is a great way to (re)connect through nurture. Make a snack together (popcorn, a bowl of ice cream with added toppings, a mixed bowl of sweet and savoury snacks or whatever your personal choice is). Bring the duvet down from a bed and snuggle up on the sofa together while you share the snack and watch a movie together. Take turns to pick a movie or make it a sofa day whereby you each get to pick a movie (their favourite and then yours). You don't have to chat – you are connecting through the close physical proximity and feeling nurtured in the snuggle, the blanket and the snack. This is a less intense way of re-establishing closeness at this time.

About estrangement: 'We are going to stay as close as we were in childhood'

Dan's story (parent)

I met with 14-year-old Mark and his dad after his dad (Dan) made contact with me to say that they wanted some sessions together to work on their relationship. In this initial session, Mark didn't say anything at all, other than shrugging and saying, 'I guess so' when his dad pointedly said, 'Isn't that right, Mark?' I observed that as his dad spoke, Mark was visibly squirming and within 30 minutes had pushed himself as far back into the corner of the couch as he could, creating a greater degree of physical distance between him and his dad. He was flushed and clearly uncomfortable. His dad had recounted the trajectory of their father–son relationship thus far in great detail. I noticed that it was idealised and bore testimony to how close they had always been.

There was a particular emphasis on a shared interest they both loved and had been actively involved in since Mark was four years old: taekwondo. The crux of the matter was that Mark had recently disengaged from taekwondo and his dad was struggling to accept this. Dan was convinced that something must have happened with some of the kids in taekwondo and that Mark was withdrawing because of bullying or some such experience. Mark was being very clear that nothing had happened; he liked the other kids but he did not want to do this activity anymore.

I reflected to his dad what Mark was clearly saying and wondered how he felt about Mark's words. He just couldn't hear it and instead reverted to insisting that Mark loved taekwondo and that it was their time together each week, adding, 'Taekwondo is our thing. We've done this together since he was four years old; he can't just stop.'

Immediately, I could see how emotional his dad felt about this and suggested to him that he and I meet alone for a few weeks before bringing Mark back in.

When we met, I empathised that it is hard for your child to change so much, seemingly so suddenly, and I wondered about his relationship with his own father as he had grown up.

'Gosh, I thought we would just be thinking of ways to get Mark back into taekwondo; I hadn't expected to be thinking about this stuff. I actually wasn't that close with my dad growing up. He wasn't really interested in the things that I did because we were so different; he was into books and I was into sports. I always wished we were closer and promised myself that I would be a different kind of dad and would have that closeness with my own son. And I've done that really well, I think, until recently... I'm just so disappointed that he's pulling away from me.'

My sessions with Dan were psycho-educational and we explored typical (albeit unpleasant) adolescent development and how this phase of estrangement was something that he had to accept and adjust to so that Mark could find himself and ultimately his way back to him. Letting Mark develop his own new and very different interests was not a sign that the relationship was fractured but that it would in fact strengthen the relationship as Mark progressed through his adolescence.

I encouraged Dan to invite in the estrangement. Instead of pushing Mark to stick with taekwondo, he put it to him that it was his decision to make but he would have to choose something else instead of it as an activity. Mark said he wanted to learn to play the electric guitar, having become interested in music, and shared that he and his friends were starting a band. Dan booked him some guitar lessons and stepped back to let Mark explore this new interest.

When Mark started to cover his room in posters and hang a blackout sheet over his window, his dad resisted lecturing him about keeping his room neat and letting some light in and instead pushed a paint brochure under his door, asking him to pick a new paint colour for his room. He then bought the paint and two brushes and together they repainted Mark's room to his tastes. We had spoken about Dan needing to find ways to create these opportunities for spending time together on an activity that met Mark where he was at with acceptance, not judgement.

15-MINUTE SOLUTION –
CREATE A PROJECT TO INVITE THE ESTRANGEMENT IN

As your child is transitioning from middle childhood into adolescence, give them the choice and chance to mark the transition by redesigning their bedroom space. If they share a room, this will need to be modified to them redesigning their half of the room. Suggest that they start to think about how they would like their space to look and feel now. Come back within a day or two of planting this seed and spend 15 minutes a day over a week on each aspect.

- 15 minutes on choosing colours – this is their choice and you simply accept it and don't judge their choice.
- 15 minutes on deciding what needs to be moved out of their room (toys, decorations, etc.) and what could be upcycled – this is a nice project for them.

- 15 minutes on making a list of new soft furnishings.
- 15 minutes on designing a schedule for getting all of this done.
- Set a budget and a time scale because this shouldn't be limitless and is a good way for them to work within your boundaries (you set the budget) while having freedom to express themselves openly (their design).
- Pick at least two items in their existing room that can be upcycled and will stay there, for example their wardrobe can be covered/painted and given new handles and perhaps their study desk too. This means you can spend time together looking at YouTube tutorials about how to do this yourselves.
- Pick up their chosen paint with two brushes and work on this together. Don't be too focused on the method but simply embrace this as time together.
- Let your teenager pick a couple of posters or images they like and get them framed and hung on their wall as a surprise at the end.
- You are communicating that you accept their need to establish an identity/look away from you and even what they used to like and you are securing 15 minutes of collaborative engagement together each day while you work towards it.
- Focus on praising their creativity and efforts – even and especially if you hate how it all looks at the end.

About abandonment: 'I will always be my child's best friend and confidante; they will always stay this close to me'

Maria's story (parent)

Maria contacted me about difficulties she was having with her 15-year-old daughter Sarah. She asked if I would work with Sarah and 'sort it out'. I suggested that I meet with Maria herself first and then explore what the best approach would be.

'Thank you for seeing me and apologies if I seem distracted today but I'm exhausted. Actually, I'm upset and exhausted. I had a huge row with Sarah in the car while dropping her at school. I reminded her that it's her grandmother's eightieth birthday this weekend and that we'll all be going to a family celebration and she just shrugged and said she couldn't come because she has plans with her friends. I tried to stay calm, I really did, and just said she would have to cancel those plans because her grandmother's eightieth birthday is a big deal for the family. She has this attitude that just drives me crazy, and she didn't even look at me as she said that I should have given her more notice instead of assuming she would be free. I must admit, I just lost my temper with her then and called her selfish and uncaring, and suddenly I was saying all of this stuff that I've been holding on to for months now. The things I work hard not to say when she gives me this attitude all just came pouring out, and by the time we got to school she was crying and saying she hated me, and I said that if she didn't come to her grandmother's party, she wouldn't be going to any of her friends' parties for the rest of the school term. It was a mess and I just can't take it anymore. We need help.'

Maria had cried the whole way to meet me after this. I acknowledged what she had said by reflecting, 'What a difficult way to start the day, for both of you.' I asked her to tell me a bit more about Sarah, and she sat back and smiled as she recalled what a lovely little girl she had been and how close they had always been.

'Until the last 12 months, when I could see she was pulling sharply away from me and the family and becoming this unrecognisable selfish, vain, uncaring girl that I hardly recognise as my daughter. I feel like I've lost my daughter and my heart is broken.'

She cried again. I passed tissues and empathised with how hard this is. I asked her if it would be okay for me to try to tell this same story but from Sarah's point of view, saying I would have to use the Sarah she described to me, as I had not met Sarah myself. I sat back in my chair and retold the story of the last 12 months, ending with that morning's argument but from the point of view of a teenager who wanted and needed to pull away from her loving parent who believed that she always knew what was best for her and still wanted to manage her life for her as she had done when she was a younger child. I talked about how I loved my mother and my family but really wanted them to leave me alone and respect that I had my own life to live and that I had made a commitment to my friends that I was being told I must break without anyone even wondering what that commitment had been. I exclaimed at Maria, 'You just don't get it, Mum; you just don't get ME,' and Maria put her head in her hands and said, 'Oh yes I do – you're ME. I was this teenager.'

I suggested that we pick up at this point the next week, and we continued to work together for another ten sessions to support Maria to deepen her understanding of the world through Sarah's eyes and to use her own empathic awareness of what it felt like to be this teenager. I aimed to strengthen her connection with Sarah and to establish new, gentle yet firm boundaries that modelled respect for Sarah having this outside life but ensuring that family time was not lost as a result of it. Maria later told me that she had picked up a Frappuccino in the café beside my office and dropped it off at the school office for Sarah at her break-time on her way home and that Sarah had thanked her, saying, 'Thanks, Mum. You know I love you, don't you?'

I think the above scenario is very relatable for any parent of a teenager. When you have had a close relationship with your child and have always been the bigger, wiser, kind adult they turned to, it can feel like the break-up of a loving relationship when they suddenly drop you, de-prioritise you and look elsewhere for their advice. It can feel as if you no longer matter and this abandonment can cause heartache and lead to simmering and often erupting tensions, as Sarah's mum detailed above.

The way to parent through this stage and protect your relationship with your teenager is to accept that abandonment is an adjustment you both have to make.

A note about the Frappuccino and why I include reference to it. A rupture in a relationship needs to be followed as quickly and authentically as possible with a repair. Sarah and Maria had parted that morning in the throes of a huge rupture and it was not in either of their interests to sit in that state of rupture all day. The session with me had allowed Maria to calm down and emotionally regulate while reflecting on what had happened from both of their perspectives. She emerged from that session with fresh thinking and a new perspective. She felt she wanted to reach out to Sarah without pulling her out of class and making a scene to do so. She knew Sarah loved these Frappuccinos and dropping one in for her would clearly convey to Sarah that she was sorry about how things had gone that morning and wanted to reconnect with her, and Sarah's response communicated that she had 'heard' this message and also wanted to reconnect.

Rupture is a normal, albeit unpleasant, part of every relationship. During any given day we will find that we are in sync with each other or out of sync with each other and, in between these two, that we are getting back into sync with each other. It is the *getting back into sync* that matters in healthy relationships. The process of getting back into sync involves taking time to consider what has happened from your own *and* the other person's point of view. Then you have to meet each other in a moment-of-meeting – a connected way to communicate that you each understand what it was like for the other person, and in doing so you reconnect. This is so important for showing our teenagers that relationships are stronger than our falling out and disagreeing. It shows them that they can make amends following a disagreement and that there is growth and learning to be found in that process of making amends. And just as when they were really young, this is still a time for growth and development as people.[2]

About control: 'I should not be challenged or resisted'

Simon's story (parent)

By his own admission, Simon 'ran a tight ship' at home. He believed himself to be fair but strict and that if you ease up at all, children, especially teenagers, would run wild. He came to me because he felt that his children resented him and he saw that they were much closer to their mother, who was easier on them than he was. He was sad that his kids seemed to keep him at arms' length and only approached him when they needed something specific, like help with their science schoolwork (he was a scientist). I asked him what his biggest fear at this point was and he said, 'That I lose them, that they don't want to know me as they grow up and move away.'

I asked about fear because so often it is fear that is lurking behind the veneer of control. Sometimes we seek control to defend against a fear that we cannot bear to think about. I was curious about his own experience of being parented both as a young child and also as a teenager/young adult.

'You might think I'm like this because I grew up in a controlling home but actually the opposite is true. I grew up in a home where there were no rules and no parents in charge. My parents were hippies who believed that children should raise themselves and will do best without restrictions or discipline that would risk limiting their creativity and free will.'

I empathised that a home and relationships without boundaries would be terrifying for a child.

'Oh, I was scared all the time and frightened of almost everything – dogs, spiders, water, even the weather. My parents' way of addressing fears was to immerse yourself into the thing you were afraid of, so they brought me to the deep end of the swimming pool and stepped back to try to force me to just swim. My fear never went, I just learned to control it as I got older.'

Control served a very important function for Simon; it helped to keep him alive and it tried to keep those overwhelming fears and uncertainty at bay.

'We were always allowed to roam free during our days and usually only went back home when we were hungry. I remember one time my siblings and I were out in a field quite a distance from our home and my youngest sister

fell from a tall tree and broke both her leg and arm at the same time. She passed out from the pain, couldn't move and we were far from home. I didn't know what to do as I didn't want to leave her, but I had to go home for help. It's one of my worst memories from childhood. While she was recovering at home, I would sit with her and feed her and read to her, and all the time I was simmering in rage against my parents because if they'd been doing a better job at parenting then it wouldn't have happened. Honestly, I think that was the turning point for me, and from then on I became more rigid and controlled in how I lived my life. I was nine years old.'

I wondered what he had felt when he became a parent himself.

'The moment the midwife placed that little baby in my arms I promised that I would make sure no harm ever came to them and that I would be a very different parent to my own. I am a very different parent to my own, but somehow I have children who also resent me in the same way that I resented my parents.'

In his desire to parent his own children very differently from how he experienced being parented, Simon was still using his parents' relationship as the benchmark for his own. We reflected on this and how it was much more important to take time to process the impact of his own experience of being parented rather than simply setting himself apart from it. Simon was really open to this and we commenced a piece of therapeutic parenting work that enabled him to process his experiences, activate his reflective functioning (recall some of what happened but from a position of fresh thinking and new perspective) and from here integrate the learning from his childhood.

The importance of parental scaffolding in raising secure and happy children

The imprint of how we experienced being parented as children resonates in how we parent our own children, even if we think we are using the early experience as a reference point of what not to do now. Simon grew up without the protection and reassurance of boundaries and limit-setting, and he was raising his children without the encouragement of independence and being able to make choices, even and especially when those choices might be poor choices, without which there can be no learning. He felt his parents inhibited his childhood and left him anxious and scared, and his own children were telling him almost the same message.

We talked about structure that is flexible and not rigid. We talked about boundaries and limit-setting that created plenty of space and opportunity for his teenagers to practice independence and choice within the safety of parental scaffolding. These are limits that are not limiting in terms of growth and development but still provide that sense of safety and reassurance that both parent and young person need.

15-MINUTE SOLUTION

Give choices – think about what you are happy for your young person to do in terms of privileges and give them the choice. Rather than starting with what they cannot do or what you are not allowing, start with, 'Yes, you can spend time with your friends this weekend. You can invite them over here and you can have use of the sitting room uninterrupted with pizzas or you can arrange to meet your friends at the cinema or you can go to a friend's house once I can call their parent to make sure they'll be there.' Your teen gets to pick *how* they spend time within your boundaries.

Another good way to play with control is to get creative with solution-focused and problem-solving thinking. This game communicates that you don't have to have all of the answers and that you celebrate their ideas and taking the lead too.

Golf-ball catcher: This is a bit like the egg game – the one where you have to find a way to package an egg so that when you drop it from a height, it doesn't break. That game is a good one to play here, but a spin on it is to take a handful of straws (at least eight each) and some masking tape. You each spend 15 minutes building something from straws and masking tape that would catch and hold a golf ball when it is dropped from a height (from as close to the ceiling as you can safely reach to close to the floor). This is a good one to stimulate creativity and problem-solving skills. It is also a good one when you want them or everyone to take a break from their screens or being alone in their bedroom. Say that they have 15 minutes to do this and then they can go back to what they were doing.

About conflict: 'I can't stand for us not to get along'

Paula's story (parent)

Paula arrived to our first session very concerned about her daughter and in particular about their relationship. Paula's daughter, Louise, was 14 years old and their relationship was not good.

'There are daily rows. She yells at me at least twice a day, and I feel like she hates me and it's breaking my heart because we used to be so close. I cannot stand this conflict, not with anyone but least of all with my own daughter.'

I asked about her role in the conflict.

'What do you mean? I don't fight back with her. I don't even raise my voice to her; it's just not in my nature. I don't say anything other than asking her to stop, and to be honest I usually end up crying.'

While conflict is a very normal, albeit unpleasant part of adolescent development, the real problem is when the parent cannot work with it. Paula deeply personalised her daughter's anger and every row that they had. She gave me endless examples of her daughter in conflict with her while she stood passively receiving her rage without engaging with her anger. Paula was conflict averse. She ran from it. She did everything she could to avoid it.

'The very sound of her anger, that screechy tone of voice just causes me to freeze and sets my nerves on edge. I literally cannot take it so I just try to shut it [her rage] out.'

We discovered that she had had some auditory sensitivity since childhood though it hadn't ever been assessed; it was more a pattern of sensitivity to loud or high-pitched noises. They really affected her and caused her anxiety-based symptoms that could last for hours afterwards, even a couple of days. Voices raised in anger, shouting and the increased pace of speech that tends to be a feature of an angry rant were very triggering for her nervous system. It wasn't that she was afraid of her daughter's feelings of frustration or anger, but she could not tolerate the sound of it. Years of avoiding raised voices and overwhelming noises had transferred into an overt expression of conflict aversion – if she avoided conflict and ran from shouting then she would not become overwhelmed by the sound of it.

Paula agreed to consult with an occupational therapist for support with her auditory sensitivity and we worked on how she could engage with her daughter's conflict without getting pulled into it or overwhelmed by it. A large part of her daughter's frustration was that she felt as if she was screaming into the wind. She felt as if she was shouting into a void and nobody could catch or contain her rage, which then spiralled out of her control.

While Paula was receiving support for her auditory sensitivity, we worked on practical things that would help her to parent without the conflict her daughter needed to provoke. We broke it down and saw that it wasn't an attack (though it might well feel like one) but was Louise's need to push her mother away to find her place in the decision-making about herself and her life. Her conflict was active and Paula's responses were passive. They were out of sync. Paula developed a line that she memorised and could easily reach for before the situation overwhelmed her. She said, 'Louise, I know that you're angry and that's okay. I even understand why you're angry. It's not okay to shout like this at me and I will walk away until things can be discussed in a calmer way. We will talk about this but not like this.' Then she would leave the room. If Louise followed her she would simply repeat this and move her space to her bedroom where Louise was not allowed. Within 30 minutes, she would have grounded and regulated herself sufficiently to go and find Louise and engage with her about what was upsetting her. She also worked with Louise about how else she could express her anger in their home.

15-MINUTE SOLUTION

Invest in positive expressions of anger:

- Encourage them to write it out – this can be via leaving you a note in an agreed place that you will read when *you* also feel calm, and then you sit and discuss it together. It can also be helpful to encourage keeping a journal or writing the feeling out in a way that can be private, not censoring, and they can write out all of the things they would like to say and even read this aloud to you or to nobody. When we read our own written words aloud we get to hear our own words and this can sound very different from thinking them in our heads alone.

- Try to deal with the issue while it is in simmer mode rather after it has boiled over – catch it when the feeling is teetering into dysregulation but not quite full-blown hyper-arousal (volcanic) state.

- Have a frustration toolkit (I would *not* be without this in my clinic or home). I have the following tools in my kit:

  - A dammit doll – this is a blobby-shaped figure, with soft stuffing that has two legs long enough to be firmly grasped by an adult-sized hand (mine is hand sewn, stuffed with old tights and has a hand-drawn face with a wool pom-pom hairdo). There is a poem that comes with this: *When you want to stamp and scream and shout, here's a little dammit doll you cannot do without. Just grasp it firmly by the legs and find a place to slam it, and as you whack its stuffing out yell DAMN IT, DAMN IT, DAMN IT!*

  - A frustration brick – this is a foam brick (looks like the one you would build a house or wall with) which can be flung and thrown in temper. Because it is foam you can experience the release in throwing 'a brick' at something without breaking anything or hurting anyone.

- ° A ball – mine is a red ball that can be taken outside and is heavy enough (so not a foam or beach-ball style) that it requires a hefty kick or throw. It is big enough to kick and small enough to throw or even hit with a racket.

- Develop an anger playlist that you and/or your child can reach for in the moment. Here is mine (of course I have one – I think we should all have one):
  1. Kelis – 'Caught Out There'
  2. Ugly Kid Joe – 'Everything About You'
  3. Eminem – 'The Way I Am'
  4. Linkin Park – 'In the End'
  5. Rage Against The Machine – 'Killing in the Name' (an anger classic)
  6. Hole – 'Violet'
  7. Nirvana – 'Smells Like Teen Spirit'
  8. Smashing Pumpkins – 'Bullet with Butterfly Wings'
  9. Skunk Anansie – 'Weak'
  10. Beyoncé – 'Hold Up'
  11. Alanis Morissette – 'You Oughta Know'
  12. Evanescence – 'Going Under'
  13. P!nk – 'So What'
  14. And now that I am coming down and want to co-regulate back to a more balanced space, my personal anthem – that song we all have that will get us up and dancing no matter where we are or how we are feeling – is Billy Idol – 'Dancing with Myself'

- Dance – just get up and start dancing (by yourself if need be) and lead by example. Dancing is a very regulating activity because rhythm and synchrony will trigger the sub-systems of your brain associated with emotional regulation.

- Go for a run or a brisk walk – some people like to run to their anger playlist. I like to sing and then dance to mine, but there is an added benefit to getting out of the house and physically distancing yourself from the heat of the situation and those in it. Also in running, you will adopt a staccato-paced movement, which is also very good to downward regulate heightened arousal.

- Draw or paint your anger – focus on what shape, size, texture, weight and colour your anger is. Add in what kind of physical environment you see your anger resting in (forest, desert, outer space, a small box, etc.).

- Try a visualisation technique – here is another one from the therapist's office. Take a chair and position it opposite and a short distance from you. You can sit or stand or a mix of both as you visualise the person you are angry with (perhaps it is yourself sometimes) sitting in that chair and you can say everything to that empty chair that you wish you could say to a person in real life.

While it is really important to have your anger/frustration/conflict toolkit, it is equally important to engage in relational repair following the rupture that conflict brings. Once you and your teenager are calmer, be sure to come back together and talk about it but, moreover, get a hug or some hand-holding in there too. Skin-to-skin touch with a safe, trusted and loved person (whom we love and feel loved by) is very effective in calming that angry nervous system and lowering those cortisol stress hormones while releasing oxytocin happy hormones. It makes us feel better from the inside out and communicates in a doing way that even though we can fall out, fall apart and yell at each other, our love for each other is stronger and can withstand all of that.

I would strongly assert that based on these essential and universal (though how they look and sound will be different in different teenagers) adjustments, conflict during this time is inevitable and actually is very important. The challenge is to engage in conflict calmly.

You engage in developmental conflict calmly by starting from a place of understanding and accepting that none of these adjustments are problems to correct; they are realities to accept. It is not uncommon to find that come their child's adolescence, many parents find that it is they who have some 'growing up' to do so that their child can grow up. This growing up of your parenting is two-fold and rooted in how you experienced being parented as a teenager and what (if any – though most of us have a few, let's be honest) unresolved issues remain. These adjustments are certainly more difficult when linked back to unresolved issues of a similar kind that parents carried into adulthood from their own childhoods. Flick back to Chapter 1 and remind yourself of your parental self-audit and consider repeating it if and when you find yourself struggling with this aspect of parenting as it may well provide the insight you need to help nudge you through this time again. The parental self-audit is intended to develop your awareness of your own triggers and issues and allow this information to inform not impede your communication with your teen.

As with any stage of parenting, try to see yourself as a *thermostat* as opposed to a *thermometer* in your relationship with your teen!

Before you simply *react*, take time out to *reflect* so that you can *respond* gently yet firmly.

15-MINUTE REFLECTION TO RESPOND RATHER THAN REACT

Hit that all-important internal pause button. Take an emotional step back from what is being said verbally and get curious.

What is the backstory of this overt emotion/gesture/action that I am seeing and hearing?

Now respond to the *power* of what is being said, rather than simply the words themselves. This enables you to respond from a position of acceptance (that this is their truth right now) and empathy (that this feeling is a struggle for them). For example:

Teenager: 'You *never* let me do anything that I want.'

Parent: 'What, *never*? You feel like I never let you do anything? Well now I get why you're yelling at me – that must feel so frustrating for you.'

Now you might want to put a gentle yet firm boundary in place.

Parent: 'I understand that you're frustrated and why you feel that way. I need to think about it some more to get to how I feel about it and it's really hard for me to think about my feelings when you yell like that. Let's take some time apart to think it all through and check in with each other about it later on before bed.'

You are stopping the tension from escalating, giving some guidance about time apart to reflect and reassuring them that you will talk some more later on when things feel calmer. This doesn't mean you will change your mind. This is about diffusing the tension when it is at volcanic levels and starting to erupt, and modelling how to manage and contain difficult feelings in the moment.

Use your time to reflect in a meaningful way. Try to *see* how they *think* so that when you revisit the topic you can do so empathically and *feel with* them, so that even a conflict can be handled within the connection of the relationship.

As a general rule of thumb during adolescence, I find it useful to keep this in mind. Thinking of your teenager as behaving badly predisposes you to think of punishment while in the moment with them. But thinking of your teenager as struggling to handle something difficult (a situation or an emotion) encourages you to seek ways to help them through their distress and struggle. This enables *correction within a connection*.

15-MINUTE EXERCISE

- Difficult behaviour is never your or your child's first choice.
- Reflect on what your first choice in any given situation would have been.
- How do you get back there instead of where you are?
  - *I'm sorry I reacted this way and said what I said. What I really wish I'd done and said is...*
  - *Will you let me try it again, doing what I wish I'd done instead?*

- Now start over with your teenager by having them tell you the thing that sparked the row and this time react in the way you wished you had.

Your teenager's behaviour is their attempt to communicate about the emotional and physical states that underpin that behaviour. The parental task is to hear and respond to the message the behaviour is seeking to communicate. When we do not see that our child *has* a problem but rather that they *are* the problem, we are not attuning to what is being said, which will leave us vulnerable to *reacting* rather than *reflecting* or *responding.*

We know that adolescence is a time of great challenge, not only for parents but also for teenagers grappling with constant and immense levels of change and challenge within themselves and their peer groups. Here are some ways to play with challenge:

Sculptionary: A spin on the game Pictionary. Pictionary itself is a fun game to play together but this variation increases the sensory experience. Everyone playing gets a lump of Play-Doh. Taking time to make the Play-Doh together first is a way of adding additional sensory stimulus to this activity. If you want teenagers to engage in making Play-Doh, think beyond the toddler variety and have a range of food dyes to colour it and perhaps some glitter to mix in as well as things like cocoa powder, essential oils or fresh herbs or lemon slices to scent it. Have a list of things written on scraps of paper and then pass the bowl around for everyone to pick one. Whatever you pick you have to try to convey by sculpting it out of the Play-Doh (so ensure you write sculpt-able words on the bits of paper as we want to encourage participation, fun and connection rather than losing them when they feel they cannot make whatever it is). Set a timer to make it more interesting (but give a good five minutes as you also want them to spend time manipulating the Play-Doh to maximise the sensory benefit). Then see if you can guess what each other's sculptures are before mushing up your own and having another round. Aim for three rounds of this game.

Cup up/Cup down: A fun and fast-paced competitive game that requires a collaborative team approach so you will need more people for this. I have done it with four people (two teams of two), but it is better with more on each team *if* you have them. Take a pack of paper cups and place an even number of them standing up and turned downwards. One team is the UP team and one team is the DOWN team. Set a timer for five minutes and explain that the objective is for the teams to each try to turn as many cups as they can up (for UP team) or down (for DOWN team) and at the end you count and see who wins. Play the best of three rounds on this one.

Napkins: A game to stimulate creativity, connection and ideas. All you need is a cloth napkin (a tea towel is fine actually) and you pass it around to everyone, one at a time. When it is your turn, you have to model a new use for the napkin beyond its intended use. It must be something original and be modelled without words at first for others to comment or guess and then the person has one minute to describe their remodelled napkin. For example, I might twist it into a neckerchief or a headband or a bracelet, which I can describe as this latest fashion must-have item, or I may drape it over my thumb and say it is a digit bandana or tie it into my ponytail and say it is a ponytail hat. The most creative suggestion wins. I like this one as it is something that you can all play together when out to eat as a family without defaulting to everyone staring into screens and ignoring each other, but you can also adapt and play it at home around the dinner table or as an after-dinner game before everyone rushes off to do their own thing.

I use play (this type of play to be precise) with teenagers regardless of age and meet with very little resistance. However, they may show you, their parent, some resistance and if that is the case, fear not because I have a simple, creative and playful solution to that resistance.

Paper snapper/Fortune-teller: You might remember making paper fortune-tellers in school – where you folded a square piece of paper into a shape that you moved in/out with fingers and thumbs, starting by spelling out a selected colour from the outside and then numbers from the inside before revealing the person's 'fortune'. Well, now I am suggesting you make an **activity paper snapper** in exactly this way and instead of writing predictions for the future inside, the final reveal will be an activity/game to play together for 15 minutes. So if/when you meet with resistance to playing, I suggest you turn to the paper snapper instead and take a chance on what it says.

Another way to use this is to keep it for creative consequences (for the mild to moderate transgressions as the bigger stuff may well require a bigger response). This would mean that a behavioural transgression sees you bring out the paper snapper that you have filled with a mix of chores and play and it's pure chance what the outcome is. Perhaps they will have to load the dishwasher or vacuum the house, or perhaps you will play thumb wrestling or bake something together. This may seem like rewarding negative behaviour but your goal is to re-establish the connection and to use it to correct the behaviour or to think and talk about the behaviour together. Remember, *connection before correction*.

CHAPTER 3

Teenage Brain Development and Risk

It is easy to misunderstand your teenager. It is even easier for them to misunderstand you. Misunderstanding fuels disconnection. When parenting an adolescent, you have to embrace the art of *understanding misunderstanding*. That is to say, using *your* developed brain to make sense of what their *developing* brain cannot yet do. I don't want you to read this chapter as a lecture on neuro-development but as a lens into the inner world of your teenager and their (often) irrational, impulsive, risky and incongruent behaviours. By deepening your understanding of the developing teenage brain, you will gain insight into their behaviour patterns and emotional fluctuations. If not about excusing, this chapter is about explaining those hard-to-understand behaviours so that you can better make sense of the world through your teenager's eyes and brain.

After toddlerhood, the brain's greatest developmental spurt happens in adolescence. The process of brain maturation in middle childhood is about synaptic pruning, whereby the maturing brain is getting rid of those synapses it no longer needs in order to create space and ready the brain for this surge in development in adolescence.

The teenage brain has the capacity of inter-connected think-ing, and adolescents can make adult decisions, so long as they are afforded the time and information to make those decisions. While their brains have this *capacity* it does not always follow suit that they will make adult-style choices and decisions. This is because of the order their brain develops in during adolescence. The adolescent brain is more dependent on the limbic system, which is the emotional centre of the brain rather than defaulting to the prefrontal cortex, which is the more rational and reasonable part of the brain. So, in the heat of the moment, their decision-making can be overwhelmed by their emotions, thus making them appear overtly impulsive and irrational in thought and action. This is the cause of significant parental frustration because you can see what they are capable of yet do not do.

The prefrontal cortex area of the teenage brain is not fully developed and will not be until a person's mid-twenties. This is the area of the brain that assesses situations, weighs up outcomes, makes judgements and ultimately controls impulses and emotions. It is also the area of the brain linked to understanding and reading responses in others.

OUR EMOTIONAL EXPRESSIONS AND THE LIMBIC AREA EXPLAINED

Given that the limbic area is in the driving seat of the teenage brain, their development is further complicated by the fact that the limbic area is itself under immense pressure during puberty. When the hormonal surges of puberty combine with the changing yet dominant amygdala/limbic area, it stands to reason that you will see a sharp rise in intense emotional expressions of everything from rage to fear and aggression (turned inwards on themselves as well as projected outwards onto others) and excitement and sexual desire. The truth of the matter is that we are *all* creatures of our limbic system. So a parent's limbic system has to be in the right place to bring the teenager's limbic system into the right place. This is the very essence of co-regulation. Sometimes, and this is always its own story in and of itself, a parent might need their own limbic system to be co-regulated to allow this to happen. If you struggle to stay regulated around your own teenager, trust that your struggle is trying to nudge you to attend to yourself *so that* you can attend to your teenager. Being able to do this is not only helpful for you as a parent but also for your adolescent because you are there to cut back the overgrown hedges so that they can see the path they must follow for themselves.

THE DRIVE FOR PLEASURE AND REWARD

Teenagers develop stronger abstract thinking skills in this stage of development, and this means that they are able to consider themselves through the eyes of another. Given how important their peer relationships are to them at this stage, it is not uncommon to see them almost obsess about what their peer group think of them, and seeking their approval is a high motivator, largely because peer approval activates the pleasure- and reward-seeking drives in the brain.

Neuro-imaging scans do show that the area of the teenage brain that is well developed is the nucleus accumbens, which is the area associated with pleasure- and reward-seeking drives. This explains a lot of what we would call 'typical teenage behaviour', especially in early to mid-adolescence. As they enter late adolescence and young adulthood, the brain has further developed (still not fully though) and they are better able to understand others and be understood by others. In early to mid-adolescence they will more often than not misread the cues and intentions of others and feel that they are misread *by* others too.

SURFING THE HORMONAL SURGE

The surge in hormones during puberty aligns with an increase in the receptors in the brain for oxytocin. While oxytocin is also that happy 'love hormone' that floods your system after having a baby (which is what leads it to be referred to as the 'bonding hormone'), in adolescence the increase in receptors for oxytocin can present overtly as increased self-consciousness (itself a feature of adolescent development anyway). They are self-conscious and self-centred because they are starting to see themselves in the world around them through an egocentric lens (not unlike that of a toddler) but in doing so, they also begin to identify causes. This is because of those developmental questions of adolescence: what kind of person do I want to be and what kind of world do I want to live in? Egocentric yes, but also an opportunity for civic participation and youth activism. Just remember that our job as parents is not to give them the answers but to support them in finding their questions.

This means that the guiding and dominant part of the teenage brain is the pleasure drive, that part that says 'do it, do it, do it' and the part of the brain that takes a lot longer to catch up is that which hits our internal pause button and asks, 'Is this *really* such a good idea? What might happen if you do X versus Y?'

So-called *typical teenage* behaviour is largely associated with risk and risk-taking behaviour. This can be to win the approval or even acceptance of peers, but they are hardwired to seek pleasure without pausing to weigh up the pros and cons of the situation at this stage of development. This is precisely why adolescence is so flammable. For the developing adolescent, the attraction to trouble and passion (risk and reward) can easily get out of control. Without that internal brake light to take a moment to weigh up pros and cons, our teenagers are motivated for reward above anything else, and risk fuels that reward drive. You will also observe that your teenager requires higher levels of risk than we adults do just to feel the same pleasure rush.

We need to make sure that we have primed our children's brains to orientate more towards positive risk-taking behaviours than negative behaviours. This will not eliminate negative risk-taking behaviours; it is about managing the level of negative risk by feeding that pleasure-seeking reward drive the thrill of positive risk-taking behaviours from as early an age as possible.

Risk-taking behaviour is a crucial component of raising teenagers. This is why you must pause to consider your own relationship to risk.

PARENTAL RISK SELF-AUDIT

Take some time to stop and reflect on your own relationship with risk. Are you more driven and motivated by reward or punishment? (Note that this is not in any way intended to be a psychological measure or assessment tool; it is purely for personal and self-reflective use.)

1. Do you feel strongly motivated by money?
2. Is it difficult for you to send a meal back or make a complaint in a restaurant?
3. If you think that something is against the rules, would it stop you doing it?
4. Does alcohol feature strongly in your social life?
5. Has a hangover ever prevented you from taking your child/teenager to their weekend activities?
6. Does how others might think/feel about you influence your actions?
7. Are you anxious or fearful in new situations? Would this cause you to withdraw from an activity/event?
8. Do you often do things to elicit praise from others, even if it is something you don't want to do?
9. If something carries an equal measure of pleasure and potential harm, would you do it?

10. How would those who know you best describe you in terms of risk – a risk-taker or a risk-avoider?

11. When you were a teenager, did you enjoy team sports? Meeting new people?

12. Do you often suggest new things to do or new ways of doing something?

13. Can you easily list three positive risk-taking behaviours and three negative risk-taking behaviours?

14. What kind of risks did you take when you were a teenager? Were you the instigator of these behaviours or a follower when someone else suggested them?

15. Have you ever shoplifted? How did it feel before/during/afterwards?

16. Have you ever been arrested? How did it feel for you? What happened afterwards?

17. Do you find it easy to speak in public?

18. Is it easy for you to ask for a promotion/pay rise at work?

19. How do you feel when you see children fall and hurt themselves? What do you do/say?

20. How do you feel/behave when attending your child/teenager's sports/activities?

Understanding your own relationship to risk, both now as an adult and reflecting back on when you were a teenager, is a helpful step in developing insight into how your teenager's behaviour makes you feel and where the root of those feelings lie.

15-MINUTE REFLECTION

- Think of a negative risk you took as a teenager. For example, a time when you shoplifted/lied/went to a place you weren't supposed to be/drank alcohol while underage.

- Recall this in as much detail as possible and pay attention to how it feels to recall it.
- Did you get caught? What was it like to get caught/ not get caught?
- Did you think at the time of what might happen in terms of risk? Can you think about what could have happened now when you look back?
- Was this a one-off risk or a pattern of risk you engaged with?
- If you could go back now, would you still do it? If yes, why? If no, why not?
- What learning can you draw from this?

Teenagers need to take risks so that they can learn and develop independent thinking. If we accept that risk-taking and rule-breaking are linked to developmental changes in the brain that serve to help teenagers become healthy, analytical adults, we can accept that a certain amount of risk-taking behaviour is necessary for adolescents to fulfil their universal need for independence, developing a separate identity and testing authority.

Of course, we would ideally like that they achieve this through as much positive risk-taking behaviour as possible. Positive risk-taking has been linked to higher levels of self-esteem and decreased risk of self-harm/eating disorders/substance abuse.

Positive risks include playing team sports, volunteer activities and making new friends outside their typical peer group. Each of these activities encompasses the possibility of failure and this is what makes them risky! Learning how to win and lose as well as how to take risks to help others are important social milestones that every teen must learn to attain.

Negative risks include but are not limited to the following:

- smoking
- drug and/or alcohol use
- stealing
- self-mutilation
- unsafe or promiscuous sex
- eating disorders
- sexting (sending explicit semi-nude or nude photos via text message)
- hanging out with a group known for trouble.

These risks appeal to teenagers because they involve the highest forms of thrill-seeking but also include the highest levels of danger and consequences. Teens who participate in negative risk-taking may be doing so for the sole purpose of experimentation, but they are also learning harmful, even deadly, attitudes and behaviours that can ultimately impact the rest of their lives.

So *how* do you parent through the risk factor? Taking risks is a fundamental part of growing up, and we have all taken them at some point in our lives and survived to tell the tale. We must try to model as many positive risk-taking behaviours as possible as teens will often mirror behaviours of their parents. So be aware of your own risk-taking behaviours. When your teen makes mistakes (and of course they will), do not remain silent on the issue. Share some of your own mistakes and errors in judgement with them, as it builds trust and enhances the connection in your relationship. We learn from the mistakes we make.

Remember that it is more difficult to grow up in today's society than the one we grew up in, and the pressures, choices and risks teens take can be even more dangerous, stressful and worrying than the ones we took a generation ago. Teens are meant to take risks, so allow them to do this; just try to make sure they're taking the *right* ones.

15-MINUTE SELF-CHECK AROUND RISK-TAKING BEHAVIOURS

- Stop, ask and answer.
- Is everything okay?
- What is going on for me right now? Where am I holding that feeling in my body?
- What is going on for my teenager right now? Where do I see him/her holding this in his/her body?

This will serve to ground you and prevent you flipping your lid. Flipping your lid in the moment is sending the logical, reflecting part of your brain, that neo-cortex, offline, causing you to sink downwards into the emotional limbic area of your brain. Now you are just yelling at each other, nobody is hearing the other person and no learning can be achieved in this interaction. It is always worth taking 15 minutes away from what your teenager has just said or done to ground yourself, allowing you to respond rather than just react to them.

15-MINUTE EXERCISE

- Bring to mind an argument with your teenager (or someone else) where you feel that you were/still are 100 per cent right. Recall this in as much detail as you can and feel it in your body again.
- Now tell that story but solely from the other person's point of view. Force yourself to only think, feel and tell it as the other person saw/sees it. You can either write this narrative down or perhaps record yourself

saying it so that you can listen back to it and hear
their story in your voice.
- Note how it feels to do this. Does it change how you
feel about that argument and the other person at all?

This is about accepting that another 'truth', separate and
apart, even opposing to your own truth, can co-exist.
However, *accepting does not mean agreeing* and that is a
fundamental point in this. To accept that someone else can
have a different narrative and experience of the same situation is a healthy position that enables empathic awareness
and connection. It will also help you when you are emotionally
stretched and trying to reason with, convince and bring a
resistant teenager to your viewpoint. Being able to empathically reflect that you understand *their* viewpoint is essential.
The important thing is that your teenager knows that you, their
parent and most important adult, understands and can make
sense of what is going on for them, *not* that you make sense
of it all. You can practise radical acceptance and empathy
without agreeing with someone else. This can be liberating
for us parents; it can also diffuse the hotbed of tensions that
the parent–teen relationship often exists on.

This is not about having to *be right* all of the time (even
when you truly are right), this is about establishing and maintaining an emotional connection that can sustain even in
these disconnects in points of view.

Connection requires daily practice to become embed-
ded into our parenting. It needs to be an active part of our
daily routine. This connection time is precisely the ethos of my
15-Minute Parenting model.

15-MINUTE CONNECTION PRACTICE

Take 15 mindfully present minutes, without interruption.

- Chat together – about something fun, something of interest to your teenager, perhaps something you heard in the media and wonder what they think about.
- Play a game – a clapping game with a rhyme, a card game, a memory game.
- Sing/learn a dance – do a Tik Tok video with them.

In addition, every day:

- Start and end the day with a five-second hug.
- Play soothing music in the house at particular times of the day – perhaps during the frenetic stages of getting ready to leave for school, returning from school/work, just before bedtime.
- Pick a TV show that you know they like to watch and become interested in it – this means that you have cause to sit together in a shared interest for the duration and frequency of that TV show, and it also gives you something to talk about in between episodes. Do not criticise or deride the TV shows they like, just find one you can tolerate and even develop an authentic interest in and watch that with them.

CHAPTER 4

Adolescence: The Age of Anxiety

It is normal for adolescents, all adolescents, to feel some degree of anxiety and even waves of recurring anxious feelings throughout their adolescence, though such developmental anxiety peaks in early to mid-adolescence usually. This type of anxiety tends to centre on the physical and emotional shifts that are occurring. This is physical appearance (how they perceive their physical appearance and how they imagine others perceive it); social acceptance (the desire to fit in and be accepted by their peer group can bring immense stress and anxiety with it); and the parent–teen conflict around asserting independence and separating themselves out from their parents.

Anecdotally, over the last decade I have observed a significant rise in teenagers presenting at my clinic with anxiety. I have also noticed a rise in the teenagers who seek the referral themselves, going to their parents having self-diagnosed themselves with anything from a generalised anxiety disorder or bipolar disorder after looking up symptoms on the internet. The anxiety is real. The diagnosis is not.

PLAY IS A LANGUAGE OF FEELINGS

Mental health means looking after what's going on in your head. Life can be tough at times for everyone, and we all go through ups and downs in our health, relationships, work and school. Adolescence is a time of lots of different changes, growing up and figuring out 'who I really am'. With so many changes going on in mind, body and the world and people around them, it's easy for teenagers to lose their way a little. That's normal. Most young people at some point believe that everyone else is coping way better and more easily with stuff they are struggling with, and it can feel as if they're the only one, but everyone feels out of their depth at some point when they are growing up and everything is changing so much. Many teenagers who experience struggles in their mental health and well-being will benefit greatly from some adolescent psychotherapy sessions.

A mental-health problem is when your negative thoughts or feelings are bothering you to the extent that they affect you on a daily basis and start seeping into your activities and relationships with others and start to change how you view the world and yourself in it. A mental-health problem that isn't sorted out could lead to someone developing a mental illness.

A mental illness is more serious/long-lasting and is diagnosed by a doctor or mental-health professional. It may require medical treatment as well as emotional support. There are many different types, just as there are different forms of physical illness. Examples include schizophrenia, anxiety disorder and clinical depression.

Let's take a closer look at anxiety, as this is the one I see and hear about most in my work with adolescents and the one I understand our state youth mental-health organisations are also seeing a huge increase in.

Anxiety is something that most of us have experienced to varying degrees and various parts of our lives. You know the feeling. It is deeply unpleasant. It is a feeling of emotional agitation and restlessness. You feel edgy and jumpy and hypervigilant in watching for signs that you are right to feel the way you do. Your teenager may experience a range of physical symptoms, such as:

- sweaty palms
- nausea
- headaches
- chest tightness
- rapid heart rate
- twitchy legs or arms
- disruption to tummy and/or bowel movements.

Your teenager may also experience overt behavioural symptoms such as:

- social avoidance
- school refusal
- retreating into a bedroom
- disrupted sleep
- emotional irritability.

We have all experienced some of this at one or other time in our lives. I do not say that to minimise the experience – it is an awful state to find ourselves in. It is, however, normal and can serve an adaptive and protective function in our lives. Your autonomic nervous system response drives the physical symptoms of anxiety you might experience. Anxiety is not fear, though the responses are similar. Fear is a natural reaction to a clear and present dangerous situation. Anxiety is when your mind and body *anticipates* potential (but not actual) danger or threat (physically or emotionally). But both fear and anxiety activates our fight/flight/freeze responses.

You can feel anxious in response to new and unfamiliar experiences. Hence it is so prevalent in adolescence when teenagers are flooded with first-time experiences. First time in a new school, first time learning new subjects, making new friends, trying out new things, first crushes/relationships, first heartbreak and even studying for exams can all illicit anxiety responses. This type of anxiety, while unpleasant, is not harmful to our mental health or us. However, it is deeply beneficial if your teenager knows that they can speak openly with you about all of this and be met with your acceptance and empathy as you sit with them in their feeling and support them in finding their way out of it with fresh thinking and a new perspective on the situation. Do not seek to minimise, dismiss or fix the issue for them. It doesn't work and actually serves to increase the anxiety for the teenager.

Whether anxiety is in the normal range of adolescent development or problematic depends on the source and intensity of the anxiety in question. Normal anxiety is intermittent and context specific, whereas problematic anxiety is pervasive, constant and impacts on all aspects of the person's day-to-day life.

The World Happiness Report (2019) reported that negative emotional feelings such as worry, sadness and anger rose by 27 per cent worldwide between the years of 2010 and 2018. Further, we have learned from such research that anxiety disorders are the most common mental illness for children aged 13–18 years old.

In the field of professional mental-health work we define generalised anxiety disorder as symptoms of excessive anxiety/worry that can relate to a variety of topics but the symptoms are present and active for a minimum of six months and are pervasive in the person's life i.e. it's more often there than not there. If you feel that this description best fits your teenager's (or indeed your own) anxiety then it is really important that you speak with your GP and seek referral to suitable mental-health professional services. Generalised anxiety disorder is complex and serious. It is a mental illness. No amount of meditation, mindfulness, yoga or colouring books and breathing techniques can (alone) be effective. This presentation requires a blend of these along with psychotherapy and potentially prescribed psychiatric medication.

I have seen a steady rise in children and teenagers referred to me for psychotherapy with a diagnosis of generalised anxiety disorder.

In fact, I have worked with children as young as nine years old with this diagnosis. This is a phenomenon that has steadily increased in the last decade. My own experience is anecdotal of course but is also in line with the research that does exist in this area.

So why are our young people so anxious and what can we do to help them? We know that brain changes increase an adolescent's vulnerability to developing anxiety. Right through early and middle childhood our children have largely been cocooned in a safer, more structured and more predictable world that has been organised and has boundaries set by us parents. Now they are learning to walk on ice as they move tentatively forward into more independent living in adolescence. Or, at least, it should be a tentative exploration, but some teenagers will career forward at great speed and find that they stumble and fall along the way. Equally though, for those teenagers who are scared to move away from us at this stage, their first steps into adolescence may also be fraught with worry and anxiety as they experience this new world with trepidation.

As the challenges, demands and changes they experience rev up, so too does the fear of failing. This primes the amygdala, the part of their brain associated with anxiety, to fire off those fight/flight/freeze responses. This is a protective and adaptive function of the brain to keep us safe in times of threat or danger *but* if we perceive threat and danger *all* the time, as is the case with any generalised anxiety disorder, what is adaptive (life-saving) can become maladaptive (life-threatening) in that the hippocampus (which I like to think of as the brain's filing cabinet where experience and memory are stored) becomes flooded with the cortisol the amygdala releases to get us to act in situations of threat. The threat is not external but internal, and we cannot run from ourselves. It is like listening to a theme tune from a horror movie except it plays inside our brains all day long. Just pause for a moment and imagine that feeling. Imagine how it would feel to be flooded with anxiety all the time and to have a horror-movie theme tune pounding away inside you all day long. Just thinking about that makes me want to lie down. If this is the lived reality for your teenager, being able to accept it as their truth and empathise with their experience is a great starting point.

15-MINUTE CALMING PLAY

When presenting something like this to your anxious teenager, do so gently but with supreme confidence that this will help them. Talk to them about how important it is to have some quick and easy techniques that they can do for themselves, by themselves, when apart from you. Share that you have used these yourself when you start to feel anxious. Suggest that you practise them together so that they know how to do these when they need to.

Toilet roll blow: Take a square of toilet paper and hold it to a wall with your index finger. Tell your teenager to stand in front of it and when you say, 'Three, two, one, BLOW,' they are to use their breath to keep the square up against the wall for as long as they can. Repeat this three times. This is the same as taking three deep breaths but the toilet-roll square gives it a playful structure.

Puffer fish/Clam/Turtle/Starfish: This is one commonly used by occupational therapists but I have always found it very helpful to encourage an anxious teen to develop some self-regulating skills when they start to feel anxious in school or somewhere away from home. If need be, your teenager can step into a cubicle in the bathroom at school and do these. These simple and playful-sounding exercises fuel self-regulation through breathing and proprioceptive (deep pressure) input into the muscles and joints. They are quick, creative and accessible wherever your teenager might be when their anxiety starts to bubble up.

- **Puffer-fish puff:** Fill your cheeks with air so that they puff out as wide as you can get them and hold for the count of five. Repeat this three to five times in a row.
- **Clam cuddle:** Cross your arms in front of your body so that each hand is holding the opposite shoulder. Give a squeeze to the count of five. Release and repeat this three to five times in a row.
- **Turtle tongue:** Stick your tongue out as far as you can and pop it back into your mouth quickly and repeat this five times. Now, reach your tongue out and see if you can reach your chin, your nose and how far can you stretch it from side to side.
- **Starfish stretch:** Stretch arms and legs apart as far as you can. If you are somewhere you can lie down, imagine you are being pulled in opposite directions as you do this. If standing up, spread your legs apart and reach arms wide apart but over your head and reach, then release. Try to hold the stretch for a count of five and repeat the reach/release move three to five times.

Cotton-ball blow: Take a scarf (or pillowcase) and hold it between you and your teenager. Place a cotton ball and pass it between you using your breath. You will find that you both fall into a synchronised rhythm to sustain it and keep the cotton ball on the scarf. You can increase the challenge in this one by using a ping-pong ball as it is lighter and requires even better breath control to keep it on the scarf.

Bubble tennis: Blow some bubbles and identify one that the two of you will try to blow back and forth a few times before it pops. This requires a gentle breath that moves the bubble enough without popping it. It will likely pop within three to five (five is a great result!) blows, so repeat it a few times.

Shared colouring: Take a colouring sheet with quite an intricate pattern. Start on opposite sides of the page and work your way to meet in the middle. Each of you will choose your own colours and can work in silence (ideally) for the 15 minutes. This gives your teenager quiet time, allows them to come out of their heads and focus on an external point *but* do that with you. This matters because maintaining close physical proximity with someone you love and trust and are truly loved by is very reassuring when you are anxious. This activity requires no responses or words, just being with each other.

A PARENT'S STORY OF PARENTING A TEENAGER THROUGH ANXIETY

Can you recall the moment when you realised this wasn't a typical phase and that something more was going on?

Looking back at our journey now with hindsight, I can almost pinpoint the day my daughter first came to me with how she was feeling. We were in the car on a long journey and she explained to me some of her feelings of worry and how she was starting to think that they weren't normal feelings. As a mother hearing this for the first time and with no experience of it I, of course, put it down to 'normal teenage angst'. But as the months went by we soon realised that this was not 'normal teenage angst'. My daughter developed severe anxiety, depression and started to self-harm with suicidal thoughts.

Can you talk me through your own feelings as you were parenting
in this unchartered territory of anxiety, depression and mental-
health services?
*Oh, I had so many feelings over the course of all of this, strong feelings
that came in waves and almost made me feel that I too was developing
anxiety and depression.*

Worry: *At first I was desperately worried about her – I mean I was
constantly worrying all day, every day. She consumed my thoughts, and
I was worried about so many things. I worried about her feeling sad
and anxious. I worried about how this would affect her development
in social and school settings. I worried about how long it would last
and if it would ever end. I worried was this the road her life was going
to take now and that this would change my gorgeous, confident and
bubbly daughter into a different person.*

Guilt: *This also consumed me! I questioned if this was because of
something I did or didn't do. I picked apart our home life to see if
I could find the reason somewhere in there. I racked my brain over
every moment of parenting her to see if I had been too emotional, too
weak, not strong enough. Could it be something in school? Was she
being bullied and I hadn't noticed? What signs of this had I missed
and should I have noticed earlier? This was followed by some deeper
reflection. I wondered if I was an anxious parent. I wondered had I
been anxious as a child or teenager myself. Had I passed this on to her
somehow? This brought me straight back to guilt and the unanswerable
question of,* **Why her? Why me?**

Despair: *There were times over the long months of referrals and
appointments and consultations with psychotherapists and doctors
when I honestly felt despair with her and with the whole situation.
We were getting all the help we possibly could, I was doing everything I
possibly could and yet things were still bad. As much as I find this hard*

to admit, there were times I wanted to scream and hide away from it all. There were times I wanted to shake her and say 'enough now'.

Tiredness: *The parenting of a child with anxiety and depression is exhausting. For any parent on this journey, you should know that this affects you as much as it affects them. It is emotionally exhausting and sometimes physically too. The night times always seemed especially tough and challenging. I used to have an alarm set at 2 a.m. and 4 a.m. so I could get up and check on her; there were other times when I would sit up with her during the night and then have to go to work the next day.*

Pride: *Out of all the others, this one consumes me more and at a much stronger level than any of the other feelings I've had and continue to have on this journey. After a massive education on the whole issue of anxiety and depression, I feel an overwhelming pride in my daughter. I am so very proud of her. She has been through a lot and she has shown such strength of character. While she has anxiety and depression, she is so much more than that. Anxiety and depression do not define her; they are a part of her. This has, at times, consumed her, but she is the most kind, caring and emotionally mature 16-year-old I know. She has dealt with this head-on and she has never concealed it, which I hope has helped break down the stigma of mental illness a bit for others. Finding the right fit with a psychotherapist took some time, and it wasn't her first or even second psychotherapist that she felt a good fit with; it was the third one we found. In spite of this, she didn't give up or say she was done with therapy. She has really embraced her psychotherapy sessions and most of all she wants to recover and is growing stronger in how she deals with everything. That's all I can ask for. I now believe and accept that this will be present in some way or another in her life and therefore in my life too, and I feel okay about that as I know that we can and will deal with it together. We're constantly learning and using the tools we're provided with. She's still*

*so young and has already been through so much in her young years,
yet she is so strong and honestly that fills me with such pride.*

Thank you for sharing your emotional journey with me. I think
your experience is so relatable and will bring so much comfort to
other parents who may be at the start or slap bang in the middle
of all of this. I wonder if you are also proud of yourself?

*Yes, I suppose I am proud of myself. If you'd asked me that question
two years ago, I would have given a very different answer as I felt
lost and like I was floundering, as nothing I was doing seemed to be
working. If I could offer some advice to other parents going through
this, it would be this:*

- *Hang in there. This process takes time and as a psychotherapist
  once said to me, **you have to trust the process**.*
- *Reach out to the people around you. You will need your support
  network now more than ever, so pull them in. When someone
  asks if they can do something to help, say yes and give them
  something to do to help you. They could pick up some groceries,
  do a school run, drive your teenager to an appointment or just
  meet you for a coffee or a walk.*
- *You will have to fight and push so take a deep breath and get
  determined. Accessing mental-health services for adolescents is
  difficult, with long public waiting lists. Even when you meet with
  a psychiatrist, their role may only be to assess, diagnose and then
  discharge with medication and suggestions for psychotherapy that
  you may have to source yourself. Keep calling, keep asking, keep
  pushing. I learned so much about the field of psychotherapy and
  all the different types of therapy that exist. Finding the right fit for
  you and your child might take time, but don't give up because the
  right fit changes everything. Call people, ask for recommendations
  and always talk with and meet the therapist yourself first.*

DEVELOPING AND NURTURING EMOTIONAL FLUENCY IN OUR RELATIONSHIP WITH OUR TEENAGERS

You will be familiar with me saying that our young and even middle-childhood aged children look to us, their safe and trusted adults-in-charge, for their emotional cues. That is mostly us parents but I also see our teenagers' teachers in a central role in this regard. The parent–teenager and the teacher–teenager relationship should be nurtured and supported through this developmental stage.

I read a really powerful opinion piece in the *New York Times*[3] by ex-teacher and journalist David Brooks in which he refers to the work of cognitive scientists like Antonio Damasio, who showed us that emotion is not the opposite of reason; it's essential to reason. He talks about how having a strong emotional connection with those we learn from supports the integration of the learning and primes the brain to accept and process that information. In this way, emotional connection serves as a motivational force in the experience of learning precisely because how we feel about something and someone informs how we know what to attune to (connect with in other words) and what we should care about and ascribe value to. It helps us to assign a value system to what and who is worth remembering. If we want our teenagers to learn, give them something to care about, to feel passionate about. Then they will learn in its truest sense. And this is about holistic learning, not just cognitive learning. Holistic learning stands to aid them in all facets of their lives and helps to build an emotional language and resilience that will help them in their relationship with those tougher emotions such as anxiety, fear and worry. Nurturing our children's and young people's social and emotional brain is crucial for all learning experiences.

Fear and anxiety keep our teenager suspended in a state of anticipatory arousal. Like emotional meerkats, their focus is darting around, seeking signs to reinforce how they are feeling, so they can feel right and justified in feeling the way they do. In this heighted state of emotional arousal, they cannot take in and process new cognitive information. So fear and anxiety compromise their capacity to learn. This is not a reflection on their intelligence, simply on their capacity to learn and make healthy, informed choices and decisions.

Brooks also refers to the research work of Suzanne Dikker of New York University,[4] which has shown that when classes are going well, the student brain activity aligns with and synchronises with the teacher's brain activity. This can have both a positive and negative effect on the student's mental health and capacity to learn because in good times and bad, teachers and students emotionally co-regulate each other. And yet we are slow to talk about the mental health of our teachers, and the impact performance measurements, overcrowded classrooms and lowering levels of funding and resources have on teachers' mental well-being and capacity to be this emotionally available to their students. They are interfacing with students who are bringing all of life's complexities and challenges to school with them. They are expected to co-regulate and teach a large group of young people bubbling with these challenges and maintain high standards of learning and, ultimately, results. It is critical that we attend to our teacher's emotional well-being so that they can attune to and co-regulate with their students and these high standards of learning can be achieved and maintained. Social and emotional learning is not *yet another thing* we should be asking of our teachers because it should be at the centre of our school communities.

PLAY TO BUILD EMOTIONAL FLUENCY AT HOME

Feelings Jenga: With younger children, I tend to play this by using a set of coloured Jenga blocks (if you cannot find them you can paint or colour in plain blocks; it's time-consuming but also a little relaxing in and of itself). On the blocks, I write a feeling word or simply make a code so that they know pink = excited, blue = sad, red = angry, yellow = happy, orange = worried, and so on. When they take out a particular-coloured block, they must share a story of a time when they felt this feeling, with as much detail as they are able to provide for that story. While they share, I am not only 'listening' to what is being verbally shared but also observing the tone of *how* it is being said and the body language with which it is being said. I will reflect back what I've heard, mirroring tone and body language. You can do this with your teenagers as well.

An alternative way to play feelings Jenga is to write across the various blocks ahead of time with statements like:

- something that annoys you
- something that makes you laugh
- something that brings you joy
- something that makes you sad
- something that makes you *really* angry
- something that disappoints you
- something you feel 'meh' about
- something that makes you cry.

You can add in anything you want. Now when either or you (or any of you if playing with more than two people) take out a block, you must respond to that statement.

A third way I adapt feelings Jenga is to build in some social-skills directions. This means that each block has a social-skill direction on it and the person who removes the block must do the social skill on it. For example:

- Turn to the person on your right and give them a compliment.
- Pick someone to say something nice to (this is about the type of person they are not how they look).
- Shake hands while making eye contact with the person on your left.
- Tell the person opposite you three things about yourself.
- Share the last joke that made you laugh.
- What colour eyes does the person on your right have?
- Introduce yourself to the person on your left in a confident tone.
- Describe your favourite meal.
- You are president of the world. What are your first three tasks?

A fourth way to adapt this is by writing fun actions to do. In this instance, you are more overtly embracing being silly together and seeking to get everyone out of their heads and down into their bodies and into the moment. Ideas for action directions include:

- kick a goal and cheer loudly
- march proudly and salute
- dance hilariously
- flap your wings and soar
- dribble then shoot a basketball
- wiggle your fingers, toes and nose
- do arm circles and flex your muscles
- paddle a canoe
- ride a bicycle
- reach your arms to the sky slowly

- applaud and then take a bow
- serve a tennis ball and swing the racket
- drive a race car and turn the wheel sharply
- twist your waist side to side.

You don't say: Write out a list of non-verbal behaviours. I like to do this on individual scraps of paper that I fold and put into a bowl for everyone to take turns selecting one without anyone else seeing what it is. Then take turns to model and interpret the meanings of these behaviours. Everyone watching can call out what they think the behaviour being modelled is and add on what emotional message it is conveying. This activity helps teenagers (and younger children, so have everyone join in) to recognise non-verbal communication cues from others.

Non-verbal behaviours can include:

- leaning back in a chair with arms crossed
- leaning forward in a chair
- smiling
- frowning
- yawning
- nodding
- resting chin in both hands
- resting chin on knuckles
- rubbing temples
- tapping fingers on the table
- looking at your watch
- staring around the room.

Expand the learning from this by gently wondering if your teenager has ever experienced a non-verbal cue that signalled to them in a much stronger way than any words? What was it and what was the message they picked up? You could wonder why the non-verbal cue was more effective than words in this instance.

Sometimes it is hard for your teenager to communicate something like this so consider starting with your own example to show them what type of thing you mean when you ask them about it. A further, somewhat light-hearted prompt might be to ask them to recall a time when *you* gave them a non-verbal cue that told them all they needed to know about the situation and how you were feeling in the moment. Ask them to tell you what in your non-verbal communication signals to them how you might be feeling.

Conversation analysis: This is another activity I often use with teenagers that I believe helps to build emotional fluency for teenagers. For this activity, you will be the speaker and you will tell the same story three times. Your story should be short but meaningful – maybe think about an incident you experienced (good or bad) or something you observed happen. Whatever story you use, ensure that you have a strong feeling about it one way or the other so that you might convey that feeling in the following ways. Don't over-egg it; try to be authentic. That said, the first time you do this *or* if you know that reading verbal and non-verbal cues is a difficulty for your teenager, maybe be obvious on the first couple of times to build up their capacity. This is not a one-off activity – you can repeat it as often as you like. It is also a great way to break down a real-life conversation or situation that has been misunderstood or where they are struggling to understand the perspectives of others.

Give your teenager a pen and paper and say that you will tell them a story three times:

- *First telling – observe my face:* ask that they carefully observe your face throughout the first telling of the story. They should note your facial muscle tone such as 'wide eyes, averted gaze, furrowed brow, drooping mouth' and also a couple of emotional inferences from this such as 'feels surprised/shocked/sad/angry/happy'.

- *Second telling – observe my body:* ask that this time they only pay attention to your body language and note it in the telling of the story. They should note their observations such as 'hunched shoulders, folded arms, twisting fingers, bouncing leg, fidgeting' and then add what emotional sense they infer from this about how you might be feeling such as 'anger, sadness, anxiety, nervous, calm, open, tense'.

- *Third telling – observe my speech:* ask that this final time they attune only to your speech but include both verbal and non-verbal traits in your speech. So they will observe and note what type of words are you using, such as 'positive, negative, strong, gentle, kind, aggressive' but also what the emotional tone of your words is as reflected in the prosody of voice – 'pitch, pace, tone, rhythm/speed' – and from this make an inference as to how you are feeling.

- Now ask that they reflect back to you how they think you are feeling about the story you just told. They might say, 'I believe that you're angry that this happened.' Accept their analysis but reflect curiosity as to how they decided this. They should be able to make reference to your facial expression, body language and the elements and patterns of your speech to support their analysis. You can reflect if they read you correctly or not, but it is more important that they can draw on these three parts to support what they are saying.

Popcorn storytelling: This starts with a kernel of a story and then develops into something bigger. It is fun for all ages. However, you will be able to grow the story up as they hit adolescence, introducing more advanced themes and expectations of a longer or more detailed narrative. This will work with just two of you or with more people. That said, this is definitely more fun with more people involved, but I have done this with just two of us plenty of times so it also works though is a little more intense.

Invite everyone to sit together but don't make this a deal-breaker as you can play this if everyone is scattered across chairs and sofas in the room but can still hear each other. Give them a starting sentence. For instance, 'Once upon a time, a tiny brown mouse…' Have each person add to the story based on what the previous person has added. If it's just the two of you, you will do one sentence each and just pass the narrative back and forth, hence me saying it is possible but a little more intense this way. This is a great game to bring the family together, to encourage some free association, which takes us all out of our heads and down into our bodies and those now moments, but it also calls for and strengthens capacity for active listening and reading and responding to the cues of others. Starting with 'Once upon a time' gives permission for anything to happen in the story, so if something silly is introduced, just go with it.

Throughout their adolescence, we are seeking to support our teenagers in developing emotional fluency so that they might grow better attuned to their own emotional needs and develop a more in-depth understanding of their inner emotional world – why they feel how they do in particular situations or in relation to particular people. This understanding will enable them to read emotional cues in others better too. They can struggle to convey their emotional state with words due to the complex nature of feelings (our own and others' and the overlapping area between these two) so they tend to over rely on behaviour as a means of communicating confused and conflicted complex emotions.

Emotional awareness: Start by giving everybody a plain sheet of paper with a variety of emojis printed or drawn on it (or you can use an emoji ink stamp set or emoji stickers). You can then simply read a variety of emotion-activating situations or (and this is how I do this) write them out on larger sheets of paper and put them on the table or floor so that everyone can walk around and read them to themselves (of course, you read them aloud if anyone has literacy or learning considerations).

There are a couple of ways of tracking how each scenario makes everyone feel. Either they note down beside the printed/drawn emojis with a tick and referencing scenario A/B/C/D, or if using stickers or stamps they can add a sticker/stamp appropriate to how they feel.

The aim here is to capture the very first feeling that is evoked by reading or hearing the scenario because being able to capture and identify our feelings as they are activated is a step towards improving emotional fluency. Another clear benefit is that being able to very quickly identify our emotions as they are cued helps to relax the amygdala (the feeling centre of the brain) from emotionally over-firing or prematurely triggering our fight/flight/freeze responses.

You can choose how much further you want to take this one. You might want to do any of the following:

- Sit and share thoughts on what came up in relation to each scenario, or one scenario in particular.
- Share what you found surprising (avoid slipping into judgement on this one!).

- Look together at where you felt the same about
  something and where your feelings didn't align –
  share something of that together.

THE EMOTIONAL INHERITANCE WE BEQUEATH TO OUR CHILDREN

The groundwork for emotional fluency starts at home with us. In my first book (0–7 years), I emphasised the importance of conducting a regular *parental self-audit* and I now encourage you to do this again. Every time we do a parental self-audit we remind ourselves that we are carrying our own parents around inside us throughout our lives. If you are co-parenting as a couple or apart, pause to consider the impact of that increase in emotional inheritance that your teenager is wading through and developing. We owe it to ourselves and to our children to give our emotional inheritance due consideration and reflection so that we are investing in *their emotional inheritance from us.*

If we want to encourage emotional fluency in our teenagers, we must nurture a landscape in our homes for emotions to grow and develop. We do this by creating a containing environment within our homes and within the parent–teenager relationship that ensures every family member feels heard, valued, respected and understood through a felt sense of patience, acceptance, empathy, tolerance and shared joy.

Sounds idyllic, doesn't it, and who wouldn't want this in their homes and relationships? But emotional fluency doesn't just happen. It is evolved and developed within the parent–child relationship from infancy right up to and through adulthood. It is not enough that we love and care for our children. They have to *feel* loved and cared for, and this is achieved when we can meet and contain who and how they are and reflect back to them our understanding and acceptance of them in this way. People thrive in the containment of demonstrative love and affection. *This* is why we *do* communication with our children and young people rather than simply *speaking* it.

15-MINUTE EXERCISE

- Consider how love and affection were shown and felt in your own family growing up.
- How did you experience that?
- How do you show and share love and affection now in your own family/relationships?
- Does this work for you?
- Does this work for your teenager?
- How do you know?
- Bring to mind three ways that you *do* love and affection in your relationship with your teenager.
- Bring to mind the last time you did this – how did it feel for you/for them?
- How does your teenager show you that they love you?
- Who else in your life is there for you who tops up your own love cup?

These don't have to be big sweeping gestures; moreover, it is the small everyday acts of love and affection that I am seeking to bring to your mind now:

- Silently bringing someone a hot cup of tea and a sweet treat while they study, work or unwind.
- Buying a copy of a magazine or saving an article you know they would enjoy and leaving it by their bedside.
- Including their favourite treat with their packed lunch.

- Dropping off a smoothie or Frappuccino at school at lunchtime.
- Giving a five-second hug at the start and end of each day, regardless of what has passed in between.
- Playing their favourite song when they are in a bad mood.
- Making eye contact and smiling in that moment-of-meeting.
- Leaving cards that praise their efforts, sharing how proud you are of them (be specific: I'm so proud of how you helped your younger brother with his maths homework; thank you for turning my bad day around for me with that thoughtful cup of tea; I know you're supporting your friend through their hard time right now and I love how kind and compassionate you are).
- Spontaneously swinging by their favourite shop or café on the way home from school.

Always say please and thank you even when being stern: 'Please do not slam your door'; 'Thank you for joining us for dinner so that we can all eat together.' Tone is vital here, as either of these statements could sound very differently depending on tone. We also show love and affection in *how* we speak, the very prosody of our voices.

We do this to teach our children how to feel what they feel when they feel it *so that* they can move beyond it with fresh thinking and new perspective, having integrated the learning, even from the most difficult and challenging of emotions.

I've had parents challenge me on this, asserting that I am encouraging their teenagers to 'wallow in their feelings' rather than 'just getting on with things'. I can understand this confusion. It stems from our own emotional belief system and our own beliefs about emotions. In order to value emotions and emotional expression, you have to have learned that there is a value in doing this.

15-MINUTE EXERCISE

- Consider how other feelings were expressed and experienced in your family growing up.
- How did your parents express anger/aggression?
- How did your parents express joy/excitement?
- What was this like for you?
- How do you wish they had expressed all these feelings while you were growing up?
- How does this influence how you express and encourage expression of these feelings in your own family now?

Strong feelings, be they positive or negative, need to be seen and treated as a central part of healthy development. Feelings are not things to be responded to with threats of consequences or directive discipline. We may need to (creatively) provide a consequence for overt behaviour but not the underpinning emotional state itself. That is to be met with acceptance and empathy and a playful curiosity that conveys clearly a desire to connect within the confusion so that you can make sense of what doesn't currently make sense together.

When we speak about, practice and even play with feelings in our homes with our children and young people, we raise young people who are more empathic and are better able to self-regulate their own emotional arousal.

15-MINUTE EXERCISE

How many ways can you come up with to describe each of the following feelings?

- anger
- sadness
- excitement
- fear.

Write a list and aim to have at least five alternatives for each feeling word. For example:

- anger – irate, incensed, furious, mad, irritated
- sadness – sorrow, melancholy, misery, distress, anguish
- excitement – animated, delighted, elated, buzzing, enthusiastic
- fear – trepidation, jumpiness, dread, foreboding, qualm.

You can repeat this for any feeling. Focus on the most dominant ones in your relationship with your teenager at this time. When we use a broad and rich emotional vocabulary we are modelling better ways for our young people to express how they are feeling themselves. Moreover, being able to speak about our emotions in a rich and detailed way is one of the best ways to self-regulate our emotional state while drawing others towards us to support and comfort us while we do. A rich emotional vocabulary is a source of reassurance and comfort in how it empowers the parent to be a stabilising presence of structure and nurture while empowering the young person to be responsible for their own regulation. We can think of this as *emotional scaffolding* in how we provide the structure for our teenagers to work out their own emotional knots.

Questions such as these below serve as a signposting system to break down an emotionally overwhelming experience into a step-by-step process that your teenager can then actively participate in resolving for him or herself.

- Can you tell me the story of what's happened?
- Can you talk me through how you're feeling about what has happened?
- Has how you're feeling about it changed since it happened?
- How do you wish you were feeling?
- What needs to change about what's happened to get you to that feeling?

Sometimes you may have to take up a more active role in this process until your teenager can see their own way through, but as soon as they can you should step out. Being more active in the process sounds like:

- Why don't you… (take some specific action)?
- I wonder what might have made the other person do/say this. Maybe they were thinking/feeling… (emotional state).
- I wonder if this is because of some confusion on both sides, because you imagine your friend is thinking/feeling X and you're thinking/feeling Y and those two just don't line up. That might be what's causing the confusion. What do you think would help clear it up?

Try not to take this too far by handing them the solution or coming across as being on the other person's side of the situation.

It is often a fine line and it is easy to cross this line even when you are trying hard not to do so. If and when this happens, take responsibility and move to immediate repair: 'I'm sorry that it sounded as if I was against you on this. That's my fault. I don't think I was being as clear as I could have been. Let me try it again.'

When you can do this, you are also modelling how to work through a confusion or miscommunication in a relationship. Always remember that your teenager has been studying you closely since birth. They know every muscle movement of your face and body, every tonal inflection or dip in your voice, every sigh (frustration or exhaustion); they are mindful of every mindless gesture you have (a twist of a strand of hair, a twitching foot, an unconscious hum, a facial contortion). They know your rhythms, sounds, movements and body cues. They are experts in how you relate to them and in anticipating what you will do or say next. Use this to your advantage. If our cues let them know how we are feeling about something, they have a momentary edge on us to change what they are doing or saying before we react. Let them. If they change what has been happening, accept the sudden shift in behaviour and move on. Everything doesn't need to be picked apart. Also bear in mind how you express your feelings for and about your teenager. Are you aware of what you are 'saying' with your body?

THE BODY TALKS – WHAT WE 'SAY' WITHOUT OPENING OUR MOUTHS

A mum and her 16-year old daughter in constant conflict

I was working with a mother and her 16-year-old daughter. They came because the constant rows and tension in their relationship were having an impact on how the entire family was functioning and Mum felt that they needed to address it for the sake of the others in the family. I heard how the motivation was for the sake of other relationships and not this one, but in that moment I just wanted to keep that piece in mind. I observed Mum's body language as she sat alongside her teenager. The sofa in my clinic room is a comfy two-seater so it is quite difficult to create significant distance between two people sat on it. Yet somehow they managed it. Both were sitting into the corners of the sofa, pushing each other away as much as they could. Mum's body was stiff and rigid. Her shoulders were raised and she held her hands in fists on her lap. Her face was tight and it felt as if she was breathing from her chest only and in shallow, quick breaths.

Her daughter quickly asked to use the toilet and I directed her to where it was, asking that she tap the door lightly when she wanted to come in. I did this to structure her return and observe Mum in the point of separation and reunification with her daughter. I was intrigued to see that as soon as the door clicked shut and the bathroom door could be heard to open, Mum's body language totally shifted. She sighed loudly, her shoulders lowered and her fists unclenched. She looked to a picture on the wall and smiled as she spoke about recognising it as one she had studied in college. A moment later there was a tap on the door and just as abruptly her body contorted and tightened again, just in time to greet her daughter.

I wondered to myself what it must be like to see such physical withholding and defence in your mother when you were in her presence. I wondered what it must be like to have to physically defend your body against your own daughter's presence. I wondered how each understood the effect they had on each other.

In a session alone with Mum I started with, 'You're much more comfortable when your daughter isn't close by.'

She started to deny this but I interjected to say that it wasn't a question but was based on what I had observed when I saw them together. Her eyes widened and she said, 'Oh goodness, you don't think she sees that, do you?' Her fear that her daughter would have felt that her mother didn't want to be near her told me that there was love here but there were also layers of defences that had been crafted over years.

Mum spoke about her relationship with her daughter always having been a difficult one. She took a deep breath, placed her hands over her own eyes and whispered, 'I do love her, but she's just not easy to show that love to.' Her body cues told me that this was deeply shameful for her and I reflected that. She uncovered her eyes and wrapped her arms tightly across her body, 'Of course I'm ashamed. A mother and daughter are supposed to be each other's best friends and I have to brace myself to spend as little time as I can get away with spending with mine, but I do love her.'

I nodded and reflected that you can love someone and not love spending time with them. She asked me how could this be so and I responded by wondering what was activated in her when she was in her daughter's company.

What emerged was a narrative of her idealised relationship with her own mother, whom she described as her best friend. They spoke multiple times a day, every day, and saw each other every other day as she had bought her own family home in the same neighbourhood that she had grown up in. She talked about only ever remembering positive things with her mother. She didn't and couldn't recall them ever fighting.

I tilted my head quizzically and said, 'Gosh, that must have been annoying.'

She laughed hysterically and then cried. She spoke of not knowing why she found my response so funny and so sad all at once. She talked about how everyone envied her relationship with her mother – 'I mean, we are best friends.*'*

I wondered about other women in her life. She had some parent friends but these were more acquaintances, and she had had friends in school but never really a 'best friend'. I wondered if the fact that her mother took this role in her life prevented other best friends from developing. She just said that she had never thought about it like that before.

She rushed to add, 'I love my mother, but I don't always love being with her.'

I nodded and reflected back her sentence and let it hang there as she slumped back into the sofa and her body hung slightly forward as she said, 'Gosh, just like I feel about my daughter… it's the same – they're the same.*'*

A mother–daughter relationship is a complex one at the best of times. When it can survive the journey through early and mid-childhood and emerge from these adolescent years, it can take on an intimacy akin to a friendship, but it can never be the same as a friendship relationship. The power balance is all wrong. A mother is in the role of parent-in-charge. She is in the role of setting and holding boundaries and limits, of judging and informing her daughter's behaviours and actions. She is one of the greatest, if not the *greatest, influences in her daughter's life and will influence the other relationships, especially with other women. But she is a mother and not a best friend.*

Mum had felt suffocated by her all-consuming mother, who brought meaning to that phrase 'killing with kindness'.

My client resented being stifled and having every need met before she even had time or opportunity to experience the need, the lack, the longing for herself. When she had given birth to her own daughter, the weight of feeling that she would have to be that same force in her daughter's life triggered fear in activating her own attachment system. And she told that with her body cues, which her daughter heard and rallied against in her demand that her mother meet her still-developing emotional needs.

This had resulted in a state of blocked or executive care. This woman provided excellent functional care to her daughter but could not attend to the over and above that emotional needs demand and call for. Her own relationship with her mother was so enmeshed there was no space for another, and to attend to her daughter's emotional needs felt as if she would be turning away from or denying her own mother.

This was the start of a lengthy piece of work that involved individual psychotherapy sessions for Mum over a number of months, followed by some weeks of therapeutic parenting psycho-education before bringing her daughter back in for some joint sessions. As our work was drawing to an end, I observed Mum look up at the door as her daughter returned from the toilet and she met and held her gaze with a smile.

MAKE KINDNESS MORE THAN AN INTERNET MEME

We are all familiar with that internet meme *If you can be anything, be kind.* I find it kind of irritating and not only because I've seen it in multiple guises, fonts and on a variety of backgrounds for so long but because I want to yell, 'No! If you want to *be* kind, then *do* kind things, often.'

Kindness isn't a light switch housed within the feeling centre of our brain or within our emotional hearts. Kindness is a conscious practice and it takes long-term practice to embed kindness as a default behaviour. This is why we need to start early and keep it up, both for our children and for ourselves.

Kindness is more than a smile, more than being polite or friendly, although these attributes certainly contribute to the overall impact of kindness. Kindness is about treating *everyone* with authentic and genuine care: compassion, acceptance and empathy. Practising kindness involves emotionally reaching out in a bid to connect with those around you in a meaningful way without guarantee that your bid to connect will be reciprocated. And so, kindness is a vulnerable process too. It carries risk: risk of rejection and risk of being hurt. Therefore, it cannot be seen as a weak action; it has to be seen as strength of character. Only strong, resilient people can put themselves emotionally out there like that. This is why only emotionally strong people can be truly, authentically kind. This type of kindness has true impact and meaning, both in the lives of others but also in our own lives. This type of kindness is much more than an internet meme; it is a movement.

The psychosocial benefits of regular kindness practice are immense. The recipient of your kindness feels a benefit and is more likely to do something kind for another as a result of how your transaction made them feel. It also releases what is commonly known as *the helper's high* because the feeling of practising meaningful kindness activates endorphins in the brain that result in you feeling a better sense of belonging, community, connection and pride. You will feel healthier, happier, be more successful and enjoy increased energy. Again, this is why kindness has to be a lifelong practice, as a one-off act or posting a meme online will not result in these psychosocial benefits. Who wouldn't want this for their teenagers, right?

If you want to cultivate the practice of kindness with your teenager, lead by positive example. Here are some everyday acts of kindness – think small, subtle and everyday rather than grandiose actions, which are harder to achieve on a daily basis:

- Hold a door open for someone.
- Offer to help someone with their shopping bags – perhaps an elderly person or a parent struggling with shopping, a buggy and a baby.
- Always smile, make eye contact and say please and thank you to anyone you are addressing – I've seen lots of people continue to stare into their phones while muttering thanks to the anonymous hand placing their coffee in front of them. Don't do that. If we want our teenagers to look up from their phones to connect with us, let them see us do the same with others.
- Give someone a genuine compliment as you walk by, without expectation that it will be returned.
- Bake cookies and deliver them to your neighbours or to a home for the elderly in your community.
- Donate to charity – in money, time, goods (there are many ways to donate).
- Sign up to charity events – a community 10km run – and all the better if you can get your teenager to do this with you as you can train for it together in the weeks leading up to it.
- Engage with people who experience homelessness – let your teenager see you saying hello, asking someone sitting on the street how they are, offering them a newspaper or magazine you've been reading or buying them something to eat and a hot cup of tea.
- Attend an awareness-raising march for a social cause you support – invite your teenager to join you but don't demand

that they do. Let them see you make a poster and be excited and passionate about what you are doing and why.

Do these as normal everyday actions. Do not flag them as big teaching moments that you talk about to hammer home the purpose or meaning because then they become a performance and not an authentic act of kindness.

15-MINUTE ACTIVITY

Create a kindness challenge. The idea is that they spend 15 minutes a day being kind, but don't overtly focus on the time, and encourage any act, even if it is a brief and quick one, trusting that the impact lasts more than the 15 minutes.

- The challenge is to do at least one act of kindness every day for a full month.
- Make a calendar wall chart to track this *and* suggest they keep a kindness journal to track the acts – one sentence to express how the act made them feel and how they think it made the other person feel, and rating their mood out of ten at the start and end of each day.
- Tell them you will do it too and at the end of each week, share your top kindness of that week.
- Celebrate the end of the challenge with a larger-scale act of kindness that you do together – perhaps skipping your daily latte each day and saving that money so that you can donate it or use to it to send flowers or a hamper of treats or buy the makings of dignity packs and deliver them to somewhere like a care home or homeless shelter.

To really extricate and embed the learning from the challenge, do a shared reflection at the end. Ask and answer:

- What were your initial thoughts at the beginning of the challenge?
- Did your thoughts about the challenge change over the course of the month? If yes, how?
- Will you maintain the daily practice of kindness every day going forward? Why/Why not?
- If yes, how will you do this?

While the daily practice should spotlight the small acts of kindness, many teenagers also enjoy big gestures and being seen and acknowledged for what they are doing, and that is also okay and to be encouraged. So if they want to fundraise for a homeless shelter and then wish to become more actively involved in that sector as a volunteer, support them in speaking with the staff at the shelter to explore practical ways they can do that while they are still adolescents. This is also a great opportunity to research and introduce youth activists from around the world and talk about the difference they can make as teenagers in our society.

Investing in emotional vocabulary and fluency and introducing kindness as a daily practice are very practical ways to strengthen and enhance your teenager's *pro-social behaviour*. Pro-social behaviour is overt behaviour that positively impacts or affects the individual as well as others and society as a whole. The practice of daily kindness is pro-social behaviour in action.

While we are talking about kindness and nurturing a rich emotional fluency in our teenagers, always go back to that point of starting with your own behaviour. Ensure that you are speaking kindly to your teenager regardless of the active dynamic in the moment. Perhaps you want to think of and learn some kind statements that you can default to no matter how you are thinking and feeling towards them on a given day. These should be general enough to feel authentic even when there is some tension between you, yet specific enough to be personal to them.

- Always remember that you have a beautiful heart capable of beautiful things.
- No matter what else is going on for you, you always find time to kick a football with your brother. I love that about you.
- I always love this time in the car alone with you; we don't have to talk because just being with you is enough.
- Making time for a hot chocolate on our way home together is the highlight of my week.
- You are passionate about the things you believe in, and I hope that you will always feel that way.
- You value your friendships more than anything else in your life. Your friends are lucky to have you.

UBUNTU

Ubuntu is the practice of showing humanity towards each other. It is an African tribal practice that upholds that *all* people are inherently good, but we can all make mistakes and poor judgements in our lives. The practice is that members of the tribal community sit in a circle around the misguided person for two full days speaking aloud only the good that they see in them.

How lovely an idea is that? I am not suggesting that your family sit around your teenager for two days telling them how great they are, but I *am* asking that you ensure you tell them something every day. This daily practice of kindness will reap huge benefits in your teenager and yourself as individuals, and in addition your relationship will be strengthened.

I do not intend to infer that without us 'inviting' or actively supporting them to express their feelings that our teenagers will not be able to feel; I simply mean that we can strengthen this process with and for them through our support. Of course, they will feel a variety of emotions, but they may lack the language and vocabulary to express those emotions calmly in a way that deepens connection with others rather than fuelling distance. Our role as parents of adolescents is to serve as their emotional road map until they can drive that terrain themselves.

CHAPTER 5

The Problem with Problem-Solving

Throughout my 15-Minute Parenting series I have encouraged you to resist jumping in to rescue your children from every struggle or problem they experience and to resist adopting a fix or change agenda in how you parent. I am very aware that this might make sense cognitively, but in those moments when you see your child having a problem or struggling, it is very difficult to resist jumping in to rescue, fix and change things. A number of parents have made contact with me after reading the first two books in this series to say that this premise makes sense to them and they believe it to be the right thing to do yet cannot seem to stay out of the rescue role long enough for their child to solve the problem themselves. They fear that they have given their child the space to solve the problem without the road map for *how* to solve it. I want to share a six-step problem-solving road map that I believe can be adapted to use with your child at any age but is especially important in these teenage years to encourage problem-solving skills in your teenager. This is a time when it is difficult for them to accept that you could possibly understand what is happening for them and when they tend to reject your input as they seek increased independence (this includes independence in thinking as much as active independence).

15-MINUTE PROBLEM-SOLVING ROAD MAP

1. Identify the problem and ensure that you both understand the issue in the same way. At this stage, try to stay focused on the issue itself – the behaviour rather than the person or the feeling. Go with statements such as:

- I noticed that you've been late home from school most days this week…
- I've seen that you're using my work tablet a lot…
- I noticed that you've passed on the last two parties in friends' houses…

2. Turn your attention to *why* this is a problem. Consider the following in how you word this next part:

- Why does this matter?
- Why is it that you need this behaviour to change?
- What do you think might happen if there is no change – what is the worst-case scenario if nothing changes?
- What is your dominant feeling about this behaviour (i.e. frustration, anger, worry, upset)?

Now put this into a statement that you can own as yours. Start what you say with 'I'.

- I want to know that you're safe when you're not at home.
- I need to know that my tablet is fully charged for work each day.
- I worry that there's a reason you're not spending time with friends.

3. Brainstorm a range of solutions. I like to make a list of three to five potential solutions but will always include one or two silly solutions along with more realistic and obtainable ones in my list. After addressing steps 1 and 2 in this process, I will flag that brainstorming solutions is next and will give some time for the teenager to compile their own list of three to five potential solutions to the problem from their point of view, which I think is fairer than me whipping out a *here's one I prepared earlier* list of solutions that I can bombard them with while they are not prepared to counter-suggest anything. Remember, avoid a fix or change agenda in how you approach this.

The reason that I invite you to mix in some sensible with not sensible solution suggestions on your list is because it invites playfulness and humour into how you approach this with your teenager, which I always find helps when addressing a problem. This is also why I suggest you open with one of the wackier solutions before moving towards something more practical. Let me give you an example of what I mean by this, given that *wacky* is quite a vague term:

- *Problem:* My teenager has been late home from school most days recently.
- *Why this is a problem?:* I worry that something bad has happened to them.
- *Brainstorm solutions:* (1) I will alert the government that aliens are real because my teenager has clearly been abducted by one; (2) My teenager will agree to call or text me when their schedule changes so that I do not worry when they are late; (3) I will agree to stay calm and curious about what might be happening for my teenager and ask them a question instead of criticising their behaviour; (4) I will call 14 of my teenager's friends and their parents if I do not immediately get through to my teenager when they are late; (5) I will trust my teenager and accept that sometimes

everyone runs late and I agree to wait 90 minutes before I contact them about where they might be.

4. Evaluate the potential solutions as they apply to *this* problem. The next step in this process is to sit with my teenager and share our solution lists so that we can continue to work through and process the problem with a solution-focused objective. Take turns to read out each solution on your lists and laugh where they are funny and silly but mark *every* solution out of 10 *as they apply to THIS problem.* I emphasise this point because there may well be a valid solution here that would absolutely work in another situation and we do not want to dismiss *any* solution but rather explore how it applies in this particular problem we are processing together.

What can happen is that you both feel that *you* have the best solution and you reach an impasse. Try to see where the overlap in these preferred solutions lies and reach for compromise. And keep in mind that an added solution might be to invite someone not directly involved in this situation to now step in to mediate you both to the point of compromise because it is not easy when you are emotionally invested in your own position on something.

5. Action the solution by framing it with structure:

- Who will do what (break down the steps of the agreed-on solution)?
- When will this start happening (agree a timeline)?
- What needs to happen as a first step towards this solution (refer back to the steps in the 'who will do what' stage)?
- How will you each know that this solution is effective and working for you both (build in a review time, i.e. give this two weeks and then check in with each other to state if it

is working or work through an additional tweak to make it more effective)?

6. Evaluate the outcome (after a few weeks) by pausing to acknowledge to yourself that this problem is no longer a row you are having with your teenager or that you feel more reassured in relation to this problem as a result of the change that you *both* actioned. Ask of yourself and then ask each other:

- What worked/didn't work?
- What could we now do differently that would further help or strengthen how we are approaching this problem?

My foundational principle when it comes to problem-solving is to seek to learn and understand and *only* then seek to move to a solution but at no point is it to 'fix' something and never to fix someone.

Embrace a mantra when it comes to problem-solving that allows you to tell and then keep telling yourself that you are seeking to *get it right* rather than to *be right*. The difference in these two outlooks is not subtle because when I seek to get something right I am open to learning, but if I am seeking to prove or assert that I am right, I speak from a very defensive position that is by its very definition closed to new learning and closed to developing any fresh thinking or new perspective on a topic.

I think so often in parenting we feel that we have to *be right* and be the authority on everything that relates to our children. This has never been truer than *this* stage of parenting when your teenager will challenge everything that you do, everything that you say and even everything that you think or thought you ever knew. Embracing a position of seeking to get it right and letting go of the desire to be right is, honestly, a parental self-care strategy at this point. But even more than the (valuable) self-care, it keeps you open to learning *from* and *with* your teenager, and that is something that we should always try to be open to so that we can continue to grow our relationship within the *cradle of connection*.

15 MINUTES' PLAY USING PHYSICAL CONNECTIONS

Partner pull-up: This works best if you are mostly at the same height/build as your teenager but actually you can try it regardless because this doesn't depend on success. Start by sitting on the ground. Keeping your bottom on the ground, pull your knees up and ensure that you are facing each other and that you are toe to toe. Reach out and hold hands; your arms will be fully extended in this pose. Now on the count of three, keep a hold of each other's hands as you pull away from each other to leverage yourself upright. Ideally you will leverage each other up. Standing facing each other, drop your hands and reach out for a hug.

Make a laughter puddle: This is not the 'laugh until you pee yourself' kind of puddle but a human puddle. One of you lies flat on the floor resting your head on a pillow. The second person lies down on the floor resting *their* head on the belly of the first person. If there are more than two of you (and this is a great one to involve as many people as possible in, including younger children at home or other adults), the subsequent people all assume the same position on the floor, lying their head on the belly of the person who lay down before them. Begin by taking long, slow, full and deep belly breaths that you all hold to a count of three before you slowly exhale. Then repeat this but very quickly exhale so that your belly and the person resting on it drop suddenly. Then revert back to slow breaths. Repeat each slow- and fast-pace breathing three times each. Now, you laugh. Start with a soft and gentle giggle building gradually up through chuckling to a full-on raucous guffaw. It will catch on and soon you are a puddle of laughter on the floor. Take time to disentangle in the reverse order to that which you started in.

You might want to start with this and as you separate out, partner up and then do your partner pull-up if you have even numbers.

We should all embrace laughter and ensure that we are sharing at least one good, authentic belly laugh together every day, because nothing works faster or is more dependable to bring your mind and body back into balance than a good laugh. What's more, it is fun, fast and free. There is truly no better way to relieve stress and tension we might be holding in our bodies, but it has also been shown to boost our immune systems and to relax our muscles. Even more, though, is that laughter has been shown to reap benefits for the organs in our body because it enhances our intake of oxygen-rich air, which stimulates our heart, lungs and muscles throughout our body while releasing those happy endorphin hormones in our brain. A good laugh together is an opportunity for shared joy, and shared joy fuels connection between people. It is like taking a shower in joy in that everyone will feel refreshed and rejuvenated by it. This play activity will also show you how contagious laughter is and this is because the very sound of laughter cues your brain to prepare your muscles to join in with the fun. Sharing a laugh together enables our teenagers to re-experience the benefits of being enjoyed by others so that they can enjoy others.

Handshake hug: I love this as a quick and simple way to physically connect when our teenagers may not feel ready or open to receiving a full-body hug from us. Face each other and each of you brings a hand up to touch each other. Press your hands against each other and, keeping your fingers pointing upwards, wrap your thumb around the other person's hand. This is a hand hug!

Adapt this into a six-part handshake. This involves each of you taking turns to add on to a handshake to make one that is unique and special between you. Let's say you start with step 1 being a normal handshake movement, then your teenager gets to add on something, for example a high five, you add on the next part, maybe a fist bump and so on until you have your six parts. Then repeat the full handshake until you know you have it committed to memory. In my experience, this takes up to five repeats in a row but this may well be different for you, and feel free to record this on your phone so you can watch it back and ensure that you know it. This is a great way to quickly connect in any moment that requires a connection top-up anywhere. You can use it to say goodbye (mark the point of separation) and when you come back together (mark the point of reunification).

What makes handshake play so effective is that it is touch based. Touch is incredibly healing following a rupture or a row. Our skin is the largest organ in the human body and we need regular, daily affectionate touch to thrive and develop as humans. Skin-to-skin touch lowers cortisol levels in the brain while releasing happy endorphins and oxytocin. You will *feel* physically and emotionally better as a result of healthy touch with people you love. It is a guaranteed way to ensure you stay connected no matter what else is going on and is also a fast and effective way to reconnect when you have had a rupture of some kind or simply when you are feeling emotional distance between you and your teenager.

Weather report: This is a touch-based playful activity that mirrors the effects of massage. Do this using your hands on your teenager's back (over their T-shirt if they prefer):

- Drum your fingertips to mimic *rain*.
- Straighten your hands and use the edges to make a chopping motion across their back to mimic *thunder*.
- Use both hands to sweep back and forth across their back while lightly blowing on the back of their neck to mimic *wind*.
- Use the palm of your hand to make large circles on their back to mimic *sun*.
- Invite them to select their favourite weather to end with and do this one for a slightly longer time.

There is an extensive and growing body of clinical research that shows the effectiveness of using touch to lower the level of stress hormones and anxiety for teenagers and even in the treatment of adolescents with depression and behavioural disorders. This research shows not only a marked improvement in the level of the symptom experienced but also improved concentration and cognitive focus for all young people. It improves emotional connection between young people and their parents and important caregivers, and because of the still-developing neuro-plasticity of the adolescent brain, teenagers will benefit greatly from these positive touch-based experiences with an emotionally regulating parent.

We tend to stop using play and playful touch with our teenagers, and a greater degree of physical and emotional distance can creep in. Using touch as an inherent part of how we bid to connect with our teenagers communicates a felt safety, acceptance, openness to being playful and empathy for our teenagers, all of which are essential components of the parent–teenager relationship and creative connection.

CHAPTER 6

Friendships in Adolescence

We know that friendship patterns change in adolescence, with an increased prioritisation of the role of peers in their lives. We also know that being able to manage these changes well is a determining factor in adolescent mental health. But what is difficult to 'know' is what qualities or characteristics contribute to the capacity to manage these changes in friendships successfully. Why do some teenagers manage their friendships well and others struggle significantly to do so during this stage of development?

One study[5] links the success of negotiating adolescent friendship to the adolescents' ego development. The term 'ego' is used in psychological language (coming from Sigmund Freud's work) to describe that conscious part of you that makes decisions, choices and assertions. It is, simply put, the 'I' in the statement. For example, 'I don't like you', 'I don't believe you', 'I know that…'

Just to really muddy the water on this, other terms that contain the word ego (such as egoistic, egocentric, egotistical and egoic) are not actually the same as ego in developmental context. The development of the adolescent ego and its impact on social and emotional development is really down to how this emphasis on the 'I' can influence our thoughts, motives, emotions and behaviours. Teenagers can appear all-consumed with the 'I' in how they are so centred around what they want to do, how they feel about a situation, what they think on a given topic, who they are/want to be and what others think of them. This can further spread into an expression of certainty that they *know* what you are going to say and do. You know that experience when your teenager asserts, before you even know what they are going to tell you, that 'I know what you're going to say but…' and then however you respond they roll their eyes knowingly and proclaim, 'I *knew* you would say that; you're *so* predictable.'

How reassuring it can be to be able to assert that you can predict with certainty how another will react to you. They might even unconsciously set up a situation with a predictable outcome (i.e. 'Can I go to an over-16s' disco even though I'm 14?' or 'Can I go to an unsupervised house party of my school friend's older sibling?') just so that they can feel 'right'. This practice certainly feeds that developing adolescent ego.

Child psychologist David Elkind refers to the term adolescent egocentrism to describe the developmental phenomena (referred to in Chapter 1) whereby there is a disparity between what the teenager perceives others to think of them and what others actually think of them. I think of it as the process of how we perceive others and the world outside us but from our own specific point of view. As an adolescent's point of view and capacity to understand the points of view of others is still very much developing, this can be a shaky foundation on which to be standing, and can lead to all kinds of misunderstandings and uncertainties. This can trigger a lot of anxiety and confusion and can cause teenagers to turn against themselves in an 'I'm stupid; no one would want to be my friend' or against others – 'They're all stupid; why would I want to be friends with them?'

Early ego development is in sharp focus during those first three years of life. Is there anyone more egocentric than a toddler, with all of their 'I', 'me', 'mine' assertions and their impulsivity in behaviour combined with very limited understanding of the minds of others? Toddlers are motivated solely by how the world feels to them in a given moment – 'because I want to'. In later development, ego is informed and shaped by a greater capacity to understand one's own thoughts while reading the thoughts and feelings of others. This reading of others' thoughts and feelings is fraught with misunderstanding, inferences and judgements, without an appreciation that inferences and judgements are, by their very nature, prone to error.

MENTALISATION

Mentalisation is the process of making sense of each other and ourselves. This is particularly relevant as part of adolescent ego development. The concept of mentalisation[6] is rooted in the ability to attribute a variety of mental states, such as thoughts, beliefs, desires and emotions to oneself and to others. It is an awareness that overt behaviours (what we do) are underpinned by our emotional and physical states (what and how we feel). It is a process of giving imaginative quality to information at hand.

15-MINUTE EXERCISE

Picture the following scene in your mind as you read this.

A parent arrives home earlier than usual from work. They turn the key in the front door and hear music playing loudly from upstairs. Looking around, they notice bags and clothes strewn carelessly around the floor. A loud thump is followed by laughter of more than one other person. They walk upstairs and open a bedroom door.

- What colour was the front door?
- What was the music that was playing?

- What items of clothing did you see strewn around the floor?
- What caused the thump?
- Whose laughter was it?
- What door did you open?
- What did you see?
- What do you think was going on in this scenario? Tell the story as you saw it.

Now, accept that you *might be right* but you *might be wrong*. I gave you very limited information and your imagination filled in the blanks. You gave imaginative quality to what I told you by picturing it in your mind using your own experiential frame of reference. You made a series of judgements and inferences about what was happening here that you might be right or wrong about.

The key with this process, and the one that I think applies right across the parenting of teens spectrum, is to *stay in a position of not knowing but seeking to better understand.* In the theory of mentalisation, this is called adopting an *inquisitive stance.* It's akin to what I described in the first two books of this series as 'wondering'. When you see, hear and observe something with your teenager, pause before you react and instead get curious and *wonder* about it. Wondering helps you to deepen your understanding of the situation, take in the perspective of your teenager and perhaps others involved and ensure that you respond rather than just react. Often what happens when we glean some small nugget of information is that we move very quickly to fill in the blanks of what is going on, leaping to all kinds of conclusions before landing on that *ah-ha I gotcha* moment. No good comes from these types of *gotcha* moments.

This process is about developing a capacity to put yourself in another's shoes, to be able to know how you view the situation/

world while keeping another's views in mind. But this isn't some new fancy concept that kick-starts in adolescence. You mentalise all day, every day. Children start to develop a capacity for considering another's point of view back in stage 2 of developmental play (see Appendix A), at approximately four years of age, by engaging in projective/narrative and small-world type of play. I flag it again here because teenagers, developmentally, have lower levels of mentalisation. They express certainty rather than curiosity about the thoughts of others, especially as they perceive those thoughts and feelings to relate back to themselves. They can be rigid, concrete and literal in their thinking.

For example: *Parent:* 'I asked you to do the dishes – why didn't you? Do it now please before I start making dinner.' *Teenager:* 'I SAID I WOULD DO IT WHEN I'M READY. GIVE ME A MINUTE!' They might even stomp out of the room and slam the door as they go. And just like you made sense of your toddler's behaviour with and for them, you will return to doing some of this again with and for your teenager so that they can better understand their own actions as underpinned by their confusing thoughts and feelings. This might now sound something like, 'You're tired (*physical state*) after a long day at school and when I asked you to do something for me before you had time to rest you felt really frustrated (*emotional state*) so you yelled at me and then slammed the door really hard (*overt behaviour*) as you walked away.' You might then want to invite relational repair through empathic acknowledgement starting with taking responsibility, 'I'm sorry that I didn't think about this from your point of view. Why don't you take some time to lie on your bed/watch an episode of your show and when you feel rested I'd love it if you could come help me with dinner.'

Do not confuse this with a parent being permissive, weak or soft. Acceptance and empathy are fundamental to a more therapeutic approach to parenting because they call on us to engage with our own vulnerability in stepping back and reflecting on what happened not only from our own point of view but also from the point of view of the teenager. They call on us to acknowledge that we might have misread a situation while considering the alternatives. They allow us to stay focused on holding our connection with our teenager at the core of how we parent them. That is an act of strength and bravery that shows our teenagers we are able to step back, reflect and repair in a calm, clear and connected way. What better way to teach them to do this themselves? If nothing else, isn't it a better option than allowing a slammed door to escalate into a screaming row with punitive consequences and a stand-off that trickles down into the entire family's evening experience?

HOW DOES THIS ALL IMPACT ON FRIENDSHIP?

It is developmentally normal and healthy for teenagers to prioritise their peer relationships above family relationships. They spend more time with their friends and often speak of feeling better understood at this stage of development by their friends than their family members. As these shifts in friendship patterns occur, you may find they are developing new friendships other than the ones they have maintained throughout childhood so far.

In childhood, friends tended to centre around common interests in activities such as playing on the same sports teams or attending the same gymnastics, judo or ballet classes. Now, shared interests stretch to include a shared attitude towards things, a shared value system and shared activities. We also see some notable gendered differences in terms of how friendship patterns shift. For girls, we see a significant rise in intimacy and sharing of very personal details with friends who are treated as emotional confidantes. They implicitly trust their friends and a breach of that trust can be experienced as a trauma. Boys are more likely to align themselves with a group of friends who validate each other's sense of self and worth through explicit actions and deeds without that same need or even urge to share personal details or form a deeper and more intimate alliance. This does not mean that boys don't want, need or respond to more intimate relationships in their lives but (generally speaking) it is not as central to their friendship formation as it is with girls at this stage of development.

While in middle childhood they migrated towards same-sex friendships, now they are drawn to more mixed friendships with a blend of males and females in their friendship groups, and sexual interests, urges, impulses and explorations are to the fore.

Friendships are very important in the lives of teenagers and should be actively encouraged. Friendships at this age help teenagers to learn important social and emotional skills, like being sensitive to other people's thoughts, feelings and well-being. Feeling understood, accepted and socially fitting in is of great importance to teenagers, and this need can only be met in their relationship with their peers. Friendships at this age provide a great sense of reassurance and emotional support and can serve as a protective factor in terms of adolescent mental health. Though friendships outside the family take centre stage in adolescence, the young people will still need your help and support to build and maintain positive and supportive friendships.

A strong and healthy parent–child relationship is a great predictor for positive teenage friendships too. So being non-judgemental, open to the choices your teenager is making and supportive as they work the impact and effect of those choices through for themselves enables you to engage your active listening (listening to what is being said as well as what is not being said but is being communicated in their bodies) within a connected relationship. This is not only beneficial for your teenager who is learning vital social skills to carry into their own friendships and relationships with their peer group but also ensures that they continue to see you as someone to turn to and lean on when they need to work something out about their peer group.

One of the most effective ways for you to encourage positive peer relationships for your teenager is to model the same in your own friendships. Parents who have active and engaged friendships of their own tend to have teenagers who have more positive and healthy friendships in adolescence. Allow your teenagers to see you supporting, reaching out to, enjoying and nurturing your own relationships with your friends because this teaches them important social skills that will strengthen and enhance how they relate to their peers while modelling that healthy friendship is a two-way thing.

This is also where you see the impact of mentalisation in terms of how your teenager is or is not able to consider a situation from their peer's point of view. How they can or cannot imagine themselves in the mind of their peer. How they are or are not able to consider the thoughts, desires or motivations behind the actions of their peers. You will see dips and even blatant gaps in their capacity to 'get it', and at times their apparent inability to read and respond appropriately to a situation will frustrate you. This is developmental – bear with it.

15-MINUTE PLAY TO BOOST MENTALISATION

1. Ahead of time, write a number of scenarios on pieces of paper. Have the start of a story prepared. It should be relatable for your teenager but not exactly something that they have experienced. For example, consider the following scenarios:

   It is Saturday night and there is a party on in the house of someone in Jane's friend group. Jane is sitting in her room at home following what is happening on social media.

Dean swears aloud before he throws his phone across the room.

Taylor redials the number again. It rings through to voice-mail for the fifth time in a row.

Have two sets on different coloured paper if you can. One stack (let's say the blue stack) is feeling statements. These should be statements such as:

- He was angry that she…
- She was angry that he…
- She was frustrated because her friend…
- He was upset that he…
- They were confused about…

On the (let's say) green stack, write out action statements such as:

- wouldn't listen
- yelled at her
- betrayed her
- lied
- didn't understand
- excluded him/her.

Have some additional details prepared on red pieces of paper. Only you hold these and if and when you feel the story could do with a plot twist, hand them a red piece of paper that gives additional detail which your teenager must now adapt their emerging narrative to include and take into account. You can reflect on how this changed the story and their understanding of what was happening and how differently they might have reacted without this extra piece of detail.

Write as many as you can so that there are lots of options for your teenager to choose from. You read out one of your starter scenarios and your teenager must complete the story by using a mix of feeling and action statements from your pile. So that they don't feel like you are just observing them, you can also join in actively and work out your own scenario. Read out what you each came up with. Stay out of judgement and just accept their version. Wonder together what else could be happening in the scenario, inviting as much detail as they will add in.

2. Read aloud a scenario. This should not have excessive detail – far from it. It should be vague and open to interpretation. For example:

Two girls are sitting side by side. They are silent as they scroll through their phones. A group of four walk by. A minute or two later one of the girls gets up and walks in the direction the group were headed. The girl left seated puts her phone into her bag and wraps her coat tighter around her.

Now invite your teenager to tell you what is happening in this scene. If needed, use some gentle prompts, such as:

- Do they know each other? How?
- What's going on between them?
- Who are the group?
- What happens when one walks away?
- How is the other one feeling? How do you know that?

When your teenager has told their version, you could share your version as to what you think is happening.

The reality is, you could be right or you could be wrong *but* what you have done is mentalise the situation by drawing on the thoughts, beliefs, desires and motivations of the characters involved to develop a story. The story stem has very little detail and excludes thoughts, beliefs, desires and motivations so that those have to come from your teenager. This is a creative way to *paint a picture with your mind* and helps teenagers to imagine what might be going on when someone acts, does or says something, while reminding them that they might be right and they might be wrong. It is good to reinforce that the key is to stay out of a place of certainty and in a place of curiosity: *I don't know for certain what's happening but I would like to better understand it.*

This is also a great way to spend 15 minutes together, playfully creating stories and engaging with each other.

Note: This is a useful technique for you to draw on as a parent now. When your teenager does or doesn't do something or you stumble across a nugget of information, allow yourself to *paint a picture with your mind* as to what is going on for them. Pause and say aloud *I might be right and I might be wrong* before entering an inquisitive stance whereby you *wonder* what is happening from the point of view of your teenager and approach them on the matter with calm curiosity. It helps to slow you down when your brain is joining up those dots before you can even consider another alternative, and helps to ensure that you reflect and respond rather than just react.

WHAT ABOUT THE YOUNG PERSON WHO STRUGGLES TO MAKE FRIENDS?

Not all teenagers have or even want/need a large group of friends. So long as your teenager is generally happy, content and emotionally healthy there is nothing to worry about. However, if your teenager is struggling with friendships and this struggle is a source of anxiety for them then you need to step in and support them in finding their way through it.

Shared interests: These are a great way for your teenager to meet other young people who share similar interests to them. Sit together and identify some new extracurricular activities that put them in contact with young people outside their school peer group. Ensure that you actively involve your teenager in this so that they are a part of choosing the activity.

Spend time with your extended family: While your relatives are not the same as friends, spending time with people beyond the immediate family is a great way to expand and grow social skills but with the comfort of familiar people. It also allows you and your teenager to observe how they cope in social situations and casual conversation, and to learn from this.

Structure a gathering: Support your teenager in organising and inviting a few friends over to spend an afternoon or evening together in your house. Perhaps this is to do some gaming, watch movies, play sport, take a trip to the local pizzeria or simply 'hang out'. If you have a teenager who struggles a little socially, having some structure to the gathering can alleviate some stress, but ensure that this is true structure, that is, flexible not rigid planning. Your role is to support your teenager in managing this themselves – if you just do it for them, there is no learning.

Keep an open-door policy at home: One of the most valuable things I recall from my own teenage years is that I always knew that I could bring anyone home without asking and that my friends, whoever they were, would always be welcomed in my home. Ensure that your teenagers know that they can bring friends home with them and that you will welcome their friends in. This doesn't mean no boundaries – you can say 'until dinner' or 'until 7.30 p.m.' or 'Fridays only' and you can say that while they don't need to ask permission to do this, you would appreciate being told in advance, even just by text, that they are bringing someone home.

Volunteering: This is a great idea in terms of building social skills and also encouraging positive risk-taking behaviour. Explore what community activity exists in your locality and discuss this with your teenager so that they can choose an area they feel drawn to and can get actively involved in, be that homeless shelters, soup kitchens, care homes, homework clubs or working with people new to the area who may want to improve their language skills. They will build social skills and also practical skills for their futures.

Regardless of the route you take to support your teenager in improving their social skills and building a social network that best meets their developmental needs, ensure that you always praise the efforts they make, regardless of how it goes. Reflect afterwards with them on what they feel worked or wish had gone differently. Role-play situations so that they get to 'think' it out loud beforehand and afterwards with you. Encourage and praise but avoid pressure or demands. Remember that they do not need to have lots of friends or to be part of a large social group. So long as they have some friends, even a couple and are generally happy and content, they are fine – good enough is good enough applies to them too.

This being said, if you feel the blocks to making or sustaining friendships are more complex and deeply rooted or if the effect of the struggle with friendships is impacting their mental health and emotional well-being, please do seek a referral to suitable adolescent mental-health services because not all difficulties can be resolved with the type of suggestions given here.

WHAT IF MY TEENAGER IS THEIR FRIEND GROUP'S CONFIDANTE?

What can start out feeling like a privileged position for a teenager – being the member of the group that everyone turns to, confides in and leans on for emotional support – can quite quickly evolve into something else entirely.

In the previous books we talked about the emotionally sensitive child. Sensitivity has traditionally been something we, as a society, look down on or seek to dismiss with comments like 'you're too sensitive' being a criticism rather than a compliment. Yet emotional sensitivity enables a person to read a room, a situation and other people quickly and effectively. Emotional sensitivity can be a huge strength. However, it is very difficult to be emotionally sensitive when still growing and developing because the capacity to filter what is your own emotional stuff and what belongs to others is very fine and fragile. It can lead to a young person becoming completely overwhelmed by the emotional resonance of those around them and unable to process the feelings of other people. Over a prolonged period of time, this can lead to increased levels of anxiety and associated symptoms, including sleep disruption, agitation, difficulty focusing and increased irritability.

Jack's story (17 years old)

Seventeen-year-old Jack presented as extremely articulate and bright with what I would refer to as an overt intellectual swagger that I found intriguing but could see that he may come across as precocious too. On the surface, everything was good. He did really well at school and had very high ambitions for his future. He had friends and a girlfriend and described his family as loving, supportive and in positive terms. I asked him, 'So how come you can't sleep, have developed psoriasis and are having panic attacks? What do you think is going on?' He told me it was a good question and said, 'You know, I think it's because I'm like you but without your professional training.' I expressed curiosity in what he meant by this and he said, 'I'm the psychotherapist for all of my friends and even for some kids in my school who aren't really my friends. Everyone tells me everything and I'm so tired. I don't think I can fit anything else into my head and I'm worried that my brain will just give up and stop working.'

He gave me a number of examples of other teenagers who were leaning on him for emotional support and how he listened and agreed to hold their problems in confidence. He spoke about how most of it was what he called the 'everyday stresses of being a teenager' but some of it was what he called 'the dark material of this field'. He said that he felt he had no choice but to hold all of that in confidence even though some of what he was holding had been an ongoing source of significant worry and anxiety, and he was concerned about the safety of one friend. He felt that it was incumbent on him as his group's therapist to hold all of this alone.

I told him that no psychotherapist agreed to hold everything in confidence because there were limits to therapeutic confidentiality, just as I had told him when we first met. I could tell he hadn't made this connection until just now. I told him that if I ever felt that someone was in danger or that someone else could be as a result of what I was told, I would have to tell someone else to ensure everyone's safety. I reaf-

firmed this to gently yet firmly remind him that he was not expected to hold 'the dark material' as he called it and that it was absolutely okay to reach out and speak to someone else, an adult-in-charge, who could help with such a situation.

We worked through the above and I supported him in reaching out appropriately and through his parents to address the concerns. But this still left us with his pattern of being his friend's emotional container. We did the following exercise together.

15-MINUTE EXERCISE

- Write a list of all you do in your week.
- Write a list of all of the people who are a part of your life.
- Now go through each item on the two lists and put an **N** for nurturing beside the things and people who give to your life and contribute positively to your happiness and mental well-being. Put a **D** for draining beside anything and anyone that pulls or takes from you and your mental well-being and happiness more than they give back. Put an **O** for other beside anything or anyone who feels more neutral in impacting in your life.
- Go through the lists and do a reflective audit on how much positive and negative energy is flowing in and out of your life.
- Are you top-heavy on giving outwards and meeting the needs of others?
- What practical steps can you now take to change this balance to better meet your own needs?

I always emphasise that relationships are about a flow of give and take and reflect that at certain times a friend might need more of us because of a particular situation or circumstance, and that is okay. This is about a general and overall sense of who and what is emptying or filling up your love cup.

This proved to be very helpful for Jack as he had a very logical and methodical approach to what was happening for him and a desire to effect change in his life. What was important was ensuring that we stayed emotionally connected to who and what was on his list so that it didn't become a distanced task of crossing things and people out coldly. I asked questions like, 'How would it feel to not have this thing/person in your life? Is there a way of modifying it/them to keep it/them there in a more positive way?' Introducing this flexibility in thinking and reflective functioning had benefits in general for Jack and in growing his capacity for healthy mentalisation.

It is hard to be an emotional container for a group of people at any stage of development but especially so when you are a teenager. If this describes your own teenager's relationship with their peers, ensure that you have ways of doing a regular emotional check-in with them to ensure they do not become overwhelmed. And play! Remember that play is a great way to lower stress levels and get us all out of our heads and into those now moments in our bodies.

15-MINUTE PLAY FOR STRESS RELEASE

Tactile play is a great way to get out of your head and into your body. Saving the bubble wrap from deliveries and having your teens use it to pop when stressed or saving small-value loose change in a jar and sitting together to sort it into piles is another way. I also keep a (halved) pillowcase bag that I have filled with soft feathers and I add something of a different texture in there (a small pebble or a cotton ball or a piece of Lego) and invite the teenager to rummage through the bag of feathers to find and, without peeking, identify what the other object is.

Solution-focused play is another way, with practical benefits too. I save some jewellery chains that have become knotted and give them to a teenager to fiddle with and try to unknot as a way of refocusing the mind on another problem besides the one in their head. Another way to do this is to tie a series of knots into a piece of string and invite them to unknot them.

Doodling or colouring is another effective way to reset an overwrought brain, or try an art technique like this one:

- Draw the letter V near the top of the page.
- At the top of each of the two points of the V, add a small circle.
- Draw a vertical hotdog shape starting at the lower point of the V and make it quite long.
- At the bottom of the hotdog, draw a much smaller and inverted (upside down) v.
- Draw a large number 3 on the right-hand side of the hotdog.
- Draw a large backwards number 3 on the left-hand side of the hotdog.
- Draw small circles in each of the curves of the number 3s.
- Now look at what you have drawn? What is it? I am hoping that it is a butterfly of some sort.

There are many ideas you can break down into such steps and the point is that your teenager has to focus purely on each of your steps to work out what you have in mind. This helps them to not think about whatever else is causing the stress. It is also fun and there can be an opportunity for a good laugh to see what they have drawn at the end, and laughter is a great way to release tension in the body.

Use storytelling: Stories offer escapism. If you have a reader, encourage reading fiction as a form of escape. Consider reading the same book so that you can think and talk about it together. An audiobook is another way to encourage escapism through story. In the very active stress moments, this may or may not appeal. So consider podcasts that are story based and invite solution-focused thinking about a problem other than their own. Something like a true-crime podcast or a podcast that offers analysis of their favourite movies, book or TV shows might also appeal.

THE TOXIC FRIEND, AKA THE FRENEMY

Sometimes and for no apparent reason or trigger, a friendship can become toxic. I have seen this happen in the teenage years time and again and am often sitting with a young person distraught and confused as to why their 'friend' is treating them this way.

I have seen many examples of this at all ages of adolescence but predominantly at that 13–15-year-old stage when some teenagers grow up and apart but still feel tied to or connected to each other, perhaps because their families are friendly or simply because they have grown up through earlier childhood stages as friends. What can then happen is that resentment emerges for the friend who wants to pull away and starts identifying with tastes, interests and people other than their old friend. The frenemy now begins to project all of that resentment – for who they used to be and their need to convey to themselves and others that they are no longer that person – *onto* their old friend. The friendship becomes toxic.

A toxic friendship can have a corrosive effect on your teenager and change how they view themselves and others. This is because their frenemy will often put them down, manipulate them, leave them out or behave in other mean and hurtful ways that they cannot make sense of.

You cannot *make* your teenager end a toxic friendship, nor should you decide for them that this is what it is. What you can do is talk about what good and healthy friendship is. You can reflect on how it feels to be in a positive and healthy friendship and talk about how friends look out for each other, want the best for each other, are inclusive and say and do kind things. You can model this in how you conduct and speak about your own friendships, how you do things to help your own friends out and how you talk kindly about other people. This will help your teenager to work out for themselves what their friendship has become and that it is not for them.

You can encourage a wide range of friends from a range of areas of your child's life so that all of their friends are not in school alone. This ensures that they have lots of experiences with friends and if they are having challenges with one group, they still have friends elsewhere to lean on and draw support from.

This is also why it is so important to get to know your teenager's friends in an open and accepting way by having them over to hang out in your home where you can observe behaviour first-hand. Be curious about how your teenager experiences their friends by using active listening and staying in that all-important *inquisitive stance of not knowing and seeking to better understand.*

It is always a good idea to give your teenager the space to work out what is happening and how to resolve it for themselves.

That said, when it comes to a truly toxic friendship, it can be very difficult to objectively see what is going on when you are so subjectively immersed in it all. You may need to step in more actively and help your teenager to find ways to change or even end this friendship for their own sake.

Help your teenager to work out what is happening exactly and then to identify what they can do and also say when this happens in the future.

15-MINUTE SOLUTION

Who/What/When/Why: Try this structured approach of breaking down what is happening in a given situation:

- *Who* is involved in the situation?
- *What* has happened exactly? Seek as much detail in the relational episode as possible? What have I done or said in response or to challenge the actions of others involved or what could I do or say to challenge the situation and people involved that would clearly convey how I am feeling about it?
- *When* did this happen and is the situation over or ongoing?
- *Why* is this happening? Why me and why now?

Breaking a situation down into its individual component parts can help your teenager to really see what exactly is happening. It can also demystify it and support a deeper understanding of the situation. It will also help you to see and better understand what is happening from your teenager's point of view. If they get stuck on any of this, usually the why question, resist the urge to jump in and rescue them from the awkward discomfort and silence and stay with them as they work this out. It is much more effective in a sustainable and meaningful way if they get to work this out for themselves. If they are really stuck and becoming anxious about it, try to proffer a perspective using your own example and not theirs. Tell a story of a similar experience you had and what sense you made of it over time and even now that you get to look back on it. Perhaps to get it started you could reflect in a calm and non-judgemental way, for example, 'I've noticed that you always seem to be angry or upset when you come home from hanging out with Alex' as this shines a light on what needs to change in the friendship and can kick-start the above process.

You can suggest that they start by telling their frenemy to STOP. Just stop! 'Stop doing that. It's really hurtful when you do/say those things and I'm asking that you stop now.' Or they can challenge the intent and meaning of the behaviour by saying something like, 'Did you mean that to sound as nasty and hurtful as it did?' This direct question forces the other person to either retract and withdraw what they have said or to double-down and own their behaviour as nasty and hurtful. An assertive and directive message like this can be surprisingly effective in catching the other person off-guard who, when confronted by the impact of their behaviour, can be told that they are not getting away with it and have been called out and exposed. With toxic friends it can be the reaction that their behaviour elicits that drives their behaviour. So using humour, assertion or an action (such as getting up and walking away every time they say something nasty or hurtful) can be a very effective way of challenging and ultimately managing it.

It may well be necessary or simply a good idea to end this toxic friendship. This has to be managed carefully to ensure that your teenager comes out of it in a secure and healthy way. Suggesting and spotlighting new friendship opportunities can be a good way to start. This would mean that they are investing in new friendships before they end the toxic one. This can be helpful in ensuring that they have a peer support network for when they do walk away from the toxic friendship, as they may lose the group, not just the one friend. Do this by suggesting they gradually start sitting with others at lunchtime. Perhaps they can join one of the school's clubs (drama, sport, debating, volunteering, etc.) Prepare yourself and your teenager for any potential fallout of ending a toxic friendship. The toxicity is likely to increase before it goes away, as a form of attack or punishment for refusing to partake in the dynamic anymore. This can look like bullying (online or in person), exclusion and harassment. If this happens, treat it seriously and respond directly and promptly by involving the school teachers/management.

At times, it might be the positive-toxic friendship that is the issue. I know that this sounds contradictory but think of a friend you may have had yourself who was really good and kind to you. They cared about you and did not behave in a nasty way towards you. However, they also inspired really negative behaviour in you. They were the friend who gave you your first alcoholic drink/cigarette/joint. They were the friend who showed you how to shoplift without getting caught – until you both got caught that is. They were the friend who suggested you both ditch school and hang out in one of your parent-free homes for the day instead. This is a more challenging toxic relationship in many ways as there are positives for your teenager in having this friend who is so invested in them, but you are concerned about the path of behaviour the friendship is paving for your teenager and need to challenge and address that.

In this kind of dynamic, you want to try to encourage your teenager to identify the problems in the friendship because if you say, 'You are NOT hanging out with Sam anymore' you make Sam an even more attractive friend to have at this stage. It is better to try in a calm and reflective way (i.e. not in the midst of a behavioural incident you are dealing with, but when things are calm, when cooking in the kitchen or driving somewhere side by side in the car) to say something like 'I notice that you've been getting into a lot of trouble lately and that each example is a time when you were hanging out with Sam. If you steal/get caught underage drinking again, it could involve the police and even youth justice.' Here you are drawing a parallel with hanging out with Sam and getting into trouble while focusing on the potential consequences for that trouble.

FEELING ON THE OUTSIDE EVEN WHEN YOU ARE ON THE INSIDE – THE TOXIC GROUP

Sometimes it is the group dynamic itself that is toxic rather than just a friend. That was the case for 14-year-old Lily.

Lily's story (14 years old)

Lily had developed a range of stress-based symptoms, from a skin rash to disrupted sleep and decreased appetite, by the time she came to see me. Her opening statement was so striking and clear that it always stayed with me: 'I hate my friends and I hate who I am when I'm with them.'

I sat back and just exhaled, holding the silence to allow that statement to linger between us. I then reflected it back to her using the same tone of voice and emotional resonance that she had when she said it. She stared at me for another minute or so of silence and I gently held her gaze. She nodded and then cried. I handed her some tissues and poured her a glass of water and wondered what it felt like to finally get to say that out loud because it sounded like something she had been holding on to with great effort. She said she had been thinking it in her head for ages and went on to be really self-critical about who she had become and how she now behaved. I let her do this as it was clear that Lily really needed to emotionally and verbally exhale, and I knew that what she needed of me in this moment was a non-judgemental and accepting active-listening ear. That is what I gave her in this first session. I didn't offer any suggestions or wonder about solutions. I just invited her to exhale, in the broadest sense of that word. She turned and said, 'Thanks for that; I feel better. See you next week.'

Lily always had a great opener in a session. Every time I saw her she started with a definite pronouncement of some sort. The second time I met her it was, 'I never laugh anymore. Sometimes I can go an entire week without laughing.' Whatever she opened with tended to set the tone and theme of what we would talk about in that session. Before she left that second week I said as she had her hand on the door, 'Hey, Lily, what condition does a noodle have when it doesn't feel good enough?' She half smiled as she said what are you talking about and I replied 'IMPASTA SYNDROME.' She rolled her eyes but I could still hear her softly laughing as she left my office.

After weeks of these thematic bits, Lily started to weave a narrative together. She talked about how she had sat beside a girl alphabetically on the first day of second-level school and they had chatted a bit and got on okay. She said that when break time came, some other girls came into their classroom and gathered around this girl and she introduced Lily to them. 'This was it really; we all just became a group and started hanging out in school and out of school. I can't even say why I'm their friend because it's not like I got to know any of them first – it just happened. The alphabet is hardly a basis for friendship now, is it?! I just keep thinking that if I had a different surname I wouldn't be in this friend group at all. Isn't that so weird? My initial decided my friend group.'

Lily's friend group were what you might call the mean girls in school. They looked down on others, said mean things about others and strutted around in a self-appointed queen-bee manner. Lily said, 'I keep thinking about the impasta joke and laughing because I am that noodle; I don't belong in this group. I hate mean girls and somehow I have to try to become one.' No one person in Lily's friend group had done or said anything directly to her and yet she felt that her only friends in school were also her frenemies. The group dynamic was the issue, not the individuals themselves.

Gradually we worked out small but significant changes that Lily could start to make for herself. She identified that her science teacher had decided to shuffle their lab partners recently to try to stop people chatting with their friends instead of focusing on the experiments. Lily was now sitting with someone new with whom she found she had a lot in common and with whom she laughed in class. She started to tell her friends that she had to sit with this new friend at lunchtime to discuss something for class and then she gradually increased this. She made herself gradually less available to her group for hanging out or doing things together and she took up a new activity outside school with this new friend and some others from other schools who all shared her interest in computer coding. She told her friends that her parents were making her take the class, which was one afternoon midweek and a Saturday afternoon each week. She said that eventually they stopped inviting her out with them and kicked her out of the WhatsApp group. Other than one comment of 'loser' when they walked past her one day, nothing much happened and she felt relieved.

Lily identified and took the above actions herself. Her work with me was focused on identifying and rediscovering who she was and what sparked joy in her life while working through the frustrations and pressures she felt she was under to blend in with a group she was emotionally disconnected from. She remained a great one for the strong statements and the last thing she said to me when we were finishing was, 'I walked in here a cool kid and I'm leaving as a computer geek – you probably shouldn't put that on your website' and I heard her loudly laughing as I closed the door.

When you find yourself worrying about your teenager's friend choices, bear in mind that while their friends have significant influence in short-term choices and decisions your teenager will make, *you* are the greatest long-term influence in your teenager's life.

The biggest changes in our children's friendships happen in adolescence, particularly between 13 and 14 years old and again between 16 and 17 years old. These are the ages in adolescence when they evolve in their capacity to think, feel, interact and understand themselves, others and the world outside and around them. This means it is not uncommon to see significant changes to their friendship groups and patterns in both of these ages.

PEER INFLUENCE – THE POSITIVES AND THE NEGATIVES

This is also known as peer pressure, but because I want to look at it through both a positive and a negative lens, I prefer the term peer influence.

To be clear about what peer influence is and is not, peer influence is when you do something you wouldn't otherwise do, because you want to feel accepted and valued by your friends. And yes, this can be a positive as well as negative action because if I start to volunteer with charities working with people who experience homelessness, that is a pro-social outcome of peer influence. Equally, if I start to focus on recycling at home and inspiring (or insisting) that the rest of the family join me in this because climate change is really important in my peer group, this is of course a pro-social benefit of peer influence. I think that it is very helpful to force ourselves to find evidence of positive peer influence in our teenagers' lives and moreover to spotlight how *they* can be the positive peer influence for others as a way of investing in emotional resilience and self-esteem *so that* they can withstand any negative peer influence that will (not might) come their way.

Negotiating peer influence is really about developing a balance between knowing how to be yourself and knowing how to fit in and be accepted by your peer group *without* compromising your own moral standards. This can be a fragile balance at times, and remember that the capacity to mentalise (understand ourselves and understand how others experience us) is still developing in our teenagers. For this reason, embrace your own role as an influencer in your teenagers' lives and I don't mean the #ad #spon type of influencer but in the truest meaning of that word. Someone who has influence can effect meaningful and sustained change in the behaviour and life of another. Think of ways that you can be your teenagers' influencer and start by considering the ways that you already are.

Negative peer influence can often be misconstrued as an image of someone *forcing* your teenager to do something they actively don't want to do. It is more likely that your teenager will *choose* to do something that goes against what they truly think and believe and want to do *so that* they feel accepted and an active part of the group they are seeking to fit in with. Because of this element of reluctant choice, your teenager may experience overwhelming levels of guilt or even shame afterwards as they try to reconcile who they are with what they just did/said.

Remember the difference between *guilt* and *shame*. Guilt is about behaviour. I feel badly about something I did or how I behaved towards another person in terms of something I said or didn't say. It is unpleasant but healthy in terms of how it enables me to feel embarrassed and regret my action so that I can make amends and engage in emotional repair with a new learning from what happened. Shame is about the person rather than the behaviour and it can be a healthy though deeply unpleasant experience. It can be a healthy level of shame if I can use it to reflect on how I am feeling about myself, about how what has happened has changed how I feel about who I am or who I could be. This means that I recognise that I have acted against my own value system or moral code and feeling badly about this will prompt me to take an action of repair to renew or restore my own sense of emotional well-being again. Toxic shame, often (though not always) the result of growing up in a trauma system or experiencing relational trauma (when the people who are supposed to love and care for you are the same people who hurt and frighten you), leads to a person feeling not that a bad thing has happened but that *they are the bad thing*. Toxic shame paralyses the process of repair, and a person will feel entrapped or locked into a spiral of shame. They will either seek to project those icky and uncomfortable feelings outside themselves by 'attacking' others or turn that attack inwards in a self-harming behavioural pattern.[7]

The shame I am talking about in the context of peer-influenced behaviours is the guilt-based (healthy) shame and not trauma-based toxic shame, but I wanted to flag the difference.

When it comes to peer influence, try to be aware of how much of your irritation about the influence a friend seems to be having over your teenager is really about your desire for your teenager to assert themselves and make choices that express who you know them to be rather than mirroring their friend's fashion, statements and actions. If your teenager dyes their hair or starts to wear clothing that makes them look like a clone of a peer, do not react, just observe. This is not going to derail their development and may be a sign that you can creatively invite expressions of their own desire and opinions on things to encourage a stronger sense of self to emerge.

A teenager who is truly happy with who they are and has developed a good understanding of themselves will always be their own greatest influencer. They may well copy some things that their friends wear or do but resist copying things that are contrary to who they know themselves to be. Do not underestimate the impact of your influence in how this plays out. You have been influencing your teenager since they were born, and even though they may well overtly reject your attempts to influence them in this stage of development, your influence thus far has already been assimilated into who they are and that is what they will default to and draw on. Be calm, be tolerant, be available and be open. You are still influencing them now if you can only model these positive responses.

CHAPTER 7

From Sex Education to Porn

Porn (and specifically the increasingly easy access to online porn at younger and younger ages) is, I believe, one of the most challenging aspects of parenting children and young people safely through adolescence. We know that our young people are watching it, seeking their sex education from it and it is ill-informing their views of sex, intimacy, sexuality and relationships. We also know that what they are (mostly) watching is the free, easily accessed content that tends to focus on degradation, violence and brutality rather than ethically produced material.

In my work with teenagers I increasingly hear how exposure to graphic, sadistic and extreme-content online porn is sending boys a terrifying message of what they should expect from a relationship, and implying that girls should be expected to do things that they and their peers have seen in this material. A teenage girl told me that having pubic hair is unacceptable and 'gross' and that if you want to get a boy to go out with you, you have to send him a naked photo of yourself to show you are 'serious' about the relationship. Teenagers I have spoken with have disclosed that they have watched all kinds of online porn that they have accessed with minimal search words including bestiality, sadomasochism, gangbangs and degrading themed pornography. These are teenagers from very healthy and normal backgrounds, because there is no 'type' of child that is more likely to be exposed to this material; it is all-pervasive across our society.

I recall sitting on a train behind two teenage boys of approximately 15 years of age who were looking at a teenage girl's social-media account on their smartphones when one said to the other, 'Check *that* out. I would so *rape that.*' This was his way of saying he found her attractive; I understand that, but it was *how* he said it that struck me. Referring to her as 'that' and not 'her' objectified the girl in question and the expression of how he was attracted to her was in terms of how he would like to rape her, not meet her, date her, talk to her but specifically rape her.

Let me share Brian's story to highlight this a little more.

Brian's story (13 years old)

Brian's parents contacted me because they wanted some advice as to how they should handle a situation that had arisen with their recently turned 13-year-old son. I had previously worked with Brian's sister and so had a pre-existing relationship with his parents. His mother said, 'Our work with you in the past has been really useful in helping us parent through lots of things that have come up over the years but this one really caught us on the hop and you were the first person we thought of. We need help with porn.'

I met with them and they told me a bit about Brian in general, the type of child he was and how he tended towards a more innocent, even naïve and sensitive nature and felt things deeply. He had come home from school and over dinner when they typically shared the highs of their days and the parts they wished they could change, Brian had shared that hanging out with his friends talking about 'boy things' had been the best part of his day. Brian had friends but tended to play with one or two others rather than a group so this shift interested his parents, who expressed curiosity about what 'boy things' included. He casually clarified that the kind of boy things they were talking about was 'raping'. A little more curiosity brought out that this was a group of ten boys all aged 12–14 years old, talking about rape in their schoolyard. Mum said that she could feel herself getting hot and sweaty and emotionally agitated but kept trying to stay in the place of curiosity and seek to understand more. She asked him what he understood by this word and he said, 'Rape is when you force a girl to do sex and then kill her.' Once again, he was 13 years old and this was a schoolyard conversation.

His parents spoke to me about how they had handled it in the moment and afterwards. Because his older sister (now 16 years old) was at the table as well, they stepped in quickly to say that this was not quite right. Rape is a very serious crime and not something to be spoken about casually so they would not talk about it over dinner but would chat with him some more afterwards. When they did, they further learned that one boy in the group had recently acquired a smartphone and had been showing them pornographic videos at lunchtime and Brian had been so excited to be included that he didn't want to say that they were looking at 'sex stuff'. Some of the pornographic content he had seen centred on rape themes. His parents told Brian that he was not in trouble for what he had seen but he was also not allowed to watch those videos anymore. They contacted the school to make them aware of what had happened as it also affected other children beyond Brian. They had done some clarification with Brain but mostly to see what else he had seen and was now aware of. They were checking in with me because they had not envisaged that they would be speaking about rape with their 13-year-old son and wanted to ensure they had the right language and 'script' in place so that they could stay anchored and calm.

We talked it through from their point of view as parents but also their personal views about pornography. We role-played it, talking about this with each other as adults and then how it would sound to have that same conversation with a young and emotionally sensitive teenage boy. Role-playing the conversation had two benefits, one being the opportunity to get comfortable talking about an uncomfortable topic, and the second being developing a supportive narrative while beginning to anticipate what additional clarifications this would require.

We focused on centring the conversation around three core pillars that they could keep defaulting back to if they felt they were veering off topic:

- *Porn is not the same as sex.*
- *Porn is acting and not real.*
- *Sex is something that should feel fun and pleasurable for everyone involved and not cause pain to anyone.*

In preparing for this conversation with Brian, we also had to bear in mind that his 16-year-old sister had also been at the table when this came up and I reflected that they shouldn't make assumptions that she too didn't now need to hear from them on this topic.

Talking about pornography with an adolescent is quite different from talking about it with a younger child. However, it is worth noting that owing to the ubiquitous nature of smart technology, the average age to first view online pornography is now 9–11 years old so you will need to start this conversation (as I flagged in my book for the 8–12-year-old age group) before the teenage years.

In adolescence, we have to accept that pornography does feature. It is often where they go to get their sex education or seek answers to some more complex questions that they believe they cannot ask their parents or would be too embarrassed to ask.

It can be helpful to frame the conversation in a general way, such as 'I was listening to somebody on the radio talking about pornography and it occurred to me that we've never really talked about it together.' And you will always find these conversations easier to start sitting side by side in the car or while out for a walk somewhere.

This is why it is also worth paying attention to the TV shows and books that our teenagers engage with, and reading and watching some of the same material ourselves to see what themes can be extracted to speak about.

We are hearing more and more about how young people are turning to the internet and more specifically to pornography for their sexual education. Teenagers are becoming increasingly desensitised to the often degrading and violent sexual content and as such teenage girls report being under immense pressure to perform (and teenage boys under same pressure to expect and seek) so called 'porn sex'. Teenage boys are talking to me about how they cannot get the same pleasure out of being with a 'real girl' as they can from watching the 'porn girls'.

This highly charged sexualisation has also altered the due weight and import given to language such as 'rape', 'slut', 'whore', 'bitch' among children and adolescents. This carries serious implications for society and how we are equipping our children to relate to themselves and each other because sexual objectification is fast killing off the capacity for sexual and emotional intimacy among our teenagers.

THE CHALLENGING CONVERSATION CHECKLIST

When talking about pornography, sex or any other such body and sexuality-related topic, check that you do the following things:

- Be honest and open in your communication.
- Practise your active listening to avoid the door slammers.
- Avoid judgement but be authentic to your own moral and belief framework.
- Avoid shaming statements.
- Accept their views as their own and a reflection of their lived experience – don't expect a teenager to think like an adult does.
- If you need to challenge something, do so gently yet firmly.
- Remember that language matters – be mindful in how you speak and challenge derogatory language your teenager might use by simply saying, 'That language isn't okay because it's disrespectful. Find another way to say the same thing.'
- From the outset, state that you want to be able to talk about this topic in an open and respectful way and invite them to correct you on some of your language if they feel that you have been offensive in any way, and you will do the same for them.

Remember that in adolescence, the pleasure-seeking, reward-driven area of the brain develops very quickly, while the area of the brain that assesses situations, weighs up outcomes, makes judgements and ultimately controls impulses and emotions takes a lot longer to fully develop, even into mid- to late twenties in fact. This area associated with reading judgements and weighing up outcomes is also the area of the brain linked to understanding and reading responses in others. So when you keep adolescent brain development in mind and then consider the teenage brain exposed to violent, sadistic online porn for prolonged periods of time, it can be worrying to think about what can happen.

This being said, let's stay grounded and rooted in what we now know when we think about this. Seven to ten years ago we were attributing the fatal and often extreme actions of a very small number of teenagers to things like exposure to violent porn and video games. Over the last decade, much research has been carried out that has established that these areas of the brain are altered in the brains of those who regularly use online pornography or access online pornography at a very young age. Studies have been conducted with brain MRIs (magnetic resonance imaging scans) by showing two sample groups, one of whom said they were regular porn users and one who rarely or never used it. When flashing a variety of images in front of the two groups, interspersed with pornographic images, it was noted that there was little or no reaction in these brain areas of the non-porn-using group whereas the same images caused the areas of the brain in the porn-users group to illuminate like Christmas lights. Further research highlighted how regular and problematic-level porn users reported needing to seek out more material with increased frequency, for longer durations of engagement and with increasingly objectifying content in order to secure the same pleasurable release over time.

More recent research into the impact of pornography and violent video games on overt behaviour of children and teenagers highlights that the impact varies and is dependent on other variables. For example, if you play violent video games, you may well experience increased adrenaline and higher emotional arousal for a period of time afterwards, but you will (generally) settle back into your window of tolerance (that is the zone of optimal emotional regulation, where you feel most comfortable). However, if you are already predisposed to aggression or impulsivity or have a particular trauma history, prolonged engagement with the same material may well contribute to you acting aggressively and even violently. Similarly, there is evidence that the more pornographic material young people view, the increasingly explicit material they seek out to achieve the same level of stimulation and the more difficult it becomes for them to develop and maintain an intimate relationship in the real world. However, this prolonged use in and of itself won't cause anyone to sexually assault someone *unless* there are other variables present, in which case it can contribute to your behaviour. It is more often a case of correlation rather than causation.

The age when accessing this material is also relevant. Some studies show that early exposure (i.e. 14 years old and younger) to pornography is linked to significantly higher levels of deviant sexual behaviour, and specifically rape. This is relevant when talking about children and young teenagers and pornography because their developing brain is still unable to fully differentiate between fantasy and reality in a consistent way and as such young people's natural developmental pathways through their gradual emerging sexuality are short circuited. They are catapulted way ahead of where they should be developmentally and they cannot process what they are viewing. It can be said that the baseline for healthy/ normal sexual desire and behaviour becomes skewed and altered following premature and/or prolonged immersion in viewing this sexually explicit and sadistic material and this then affects how teenagers form and develop their intimate relationships.

Stay curious about and interested in what interests your teenagers. Gently, yet firmly, challenge behaviour patterns that you view as worrisome and/or problematic. Keep an open communication policy about talking about things like sex and porn and convey clearly that no topics are off limits with you. If you have concerns about your teenagers' sexual behaviours or their level of engagement with pornography, please consult with a suitably qualified mental health professional who can provide appropriate support.

KNOW YOUR LGBTQ ALPHABET

Do you know your LGBTQ alphabet and understand its meaning beyond acronyms and a string of letters? Being informed about the new landscape of gender and sexuality is vital in parenting teenagers. There is a significant change in terms of how teenagers now experience their sexuality and gender identity than was the case even a generation ago. In a 2015 YouGov survey, half (49%) of young people aged 18–24 said they did not see themselves as 100 per cent heterosexual.[8] What was once (not that long ago) a question of identifying as 'gay or straight' is now much more nuanced, complex, rich and inclusive. It is very easy to get this wrong. To misunderstand, misconstrue and miscommunicate is almost inevitable, but this is helped if you can go back to that place of *not knowing yet seeking to understand*. This requires that you assume this to be an area that you are far less informed about than your teenager is and ask them to teach. This is not to say that *all* teenagers are open-minded about sexuality and gender identity – I know this not to be the case. But it is a good place to start by checking in with your teenager as to what their understanding, views and position on this topic are.

Then there is the language itself. Many of us are familiar with hearing LGBTQ+ but not all of us will be familiar with what specifically the + stands for. Let's break that down a bit now.

LGBTQQTIAAP2S, that is to say:

- *Lesbian* – a woman who is primarily attracted to women.
- *Gay* – a man who is primarily attracted to men but also can be a term for any individual who primarily is attracted to people of the same sex.
- *Bisexual* – an individual who is attracted to people of their own and also opposite sex.
- *Transgender* – a person whose gender identity differs from their assigned sex at birth.

- *Queer* – an umbrella term to be more inclusive of the many identities and variations that make up the LGBTQ+ community.
- *Questioning* – the process of exploring and discovering one's own sexual orientation, gender identity and/or gender expression.
- *Transsexual* – now considered quite an outdated term that is rooted in medical and psychological jargon to describe someone who has permanently changed their gender identity through surgery and hormones.
- *Intersex* – an individual whose sexual anatomy or chromosomes do not fit with the traditional markers of 'female' or 'male'.
- *Asexual* – an individual who generally does not feel sexual desire or attraction to any group of people. This is not the same as celibacy and encompasses a number of sub-groups.
- *Ally* – an individual who is typically (though not exclusively) non-queer and actively supports and advocates for the queer community. Of course, an individual within the broader LGBTQ+ community can also identify as an ally for another member of the broader LGBTQ+ community who identifies differently from them.
- *Pansexual* – an individual who experiences sexual, romantic, physical and/or spiritual/emotional attraction to members of all gender identities/expressions as opposed to people who fit into the standard gender binary.
- *2-Spirit* – this is a term that originated in indigenous North American communities to describe native people within their communities who identify as having both a masculine and feminine spirit.

A less formal and more fun and relaxed way to go through all of this with your teenager might be to watch a video about it together.

Perhaps inform yourself by watching it first though. In 2017, the National Youth Theatre of Great Britain made a short 15-minute film that talks through each of the terms in the LGBTQ+ alphabet and I would recommend it as something worth watching.[9] Using multimedia as a means of framing and kick-starting a discussion can take some of the intensity and pressure off you feeling you have to have all your information and points ready to go, which in itself can make it sound like a lecture or an interrogation.

One aspect of the LGBTQ+ spectrum of identities which I would like to specifically reflect on is the 'questioning' label as I really don't think we amplify this aspect of gender and sexual identity nearly enough, but it is really appropriate to this stage of development. As I have already mentioned, our teenagers are very much still evolving and developing their sense of self throughout adolescence. Further, their brain's capacity to consider the long-term consequences and outcomes as part of a decision-making process is very much still developing and can lead to them being impulsive and desire thrill-seeking in their actions and choices. To question and sit in a place of questioning over one's sexual and gender identity at this stage of development is perfectly healthy, normal and even to be expected and welcomed. As they are questioning, wondering and exploring, it is also very healthy that they might identify in many ways before finding the sexual and gender identity that best fits them. Our teenagers do not need instruction from us parents in this regard, but they do need our support and emotional holding capacity and to know that we are available for them as they negotiate through this stage of their development.

Over the course of the last decade of my work, I have observed a growing number of teenagers who are increasingly comfortable in exploring and expressing some same-sex desire or who question their own gender identity and are reflective and critical of gender norms as they see them represented in our society. The internet has opened them up to a world of uncensored information that has expanded knowledge and awareness of the gender spectrum, and young people from anywhere in the world can find a community of like-minded people to connect with and can feel less isolated and alone in their sexual and gender identity journey. We are also seeing more positive representation of transgender role models in our media, such as Laverne Cox, Janet Mock and Paris Lees, with many other celebrities serving as allies to the LGBTQ+ community by using their own social media to amplify and champion cultural tolerance, information and new voices from the LGBTQ+ community.

This is great and certainly a positive of the internet. Adolescents are now growing up in a society that empowers them to explore and try on labels that are more reflective of their sexual and gender fantasies, experiences and their developing sense of self.

We are still aware of how difficult it can be for young people who identify in a way other than heteronormative. Even as our global society evolves, we still see evidence that LGBTQ+ teenagers are more likely to experience mental-health struggles and to drop out or take time out of education as a direct result of sexual and gender identity.[10] In my own clinical practice, I still meet teenagers and young adults who present with active levels of trauma, shame, guilt and remnants of internalised beliefs or hostility towards their own gender and sexual identity. As many political campaign statements go, we may have a lot done in this regard but my goodness we certainly have a lot more to do.

As with so many aspects of parenting, when it comes to parenting within an LGBTQ+ framework, start with yourself and your own internalised biases and views:

1. Don't underestimate your unconscious and bring a conscious awareness to your own beliefs and assumptions about gender and sexual identity. Reflect on your sexual and gender identity beliefs and how this influences your own relationship style.

2. Start from a place of 'not knowing but seeking to better understand' and educate yourself on LGBTQ+ matters.

3. Be open but be honest about your limits. You can be open and seek to understand while honestly sharing that you feel out of your depth and that parts of a discussion with your teenager or this topic make you feel uncomfortable and are personally challenging for you. This can be within the context of still needing to learn and understand this more or it may be that your own religious or moral code feels that it is limiting how far you can go in terms of open acceptance on this topic. This is your struggle and not to be put on your teenager as their issue. Just because you struggle doesn't mean they are wrong and need to change. Being in a place of struggle is not comfortable or easy for anyone, and you may well benefit from consulting with an informed psychotherapist on this matter to support you to support your teenager without feeling compromised within your belief system.

4. Actively show your openness or willingness to learn and discuss these matters by having appropriate literature and information on LGBTQ+ matters in your home. Acknowledge events like Pride or marriage equality votes around the world. These actions don't mean that you necessarily fully support any particular aspect of this cause (or any other) but it is about letting your teenager know that they can talk about such things openly with you.

5. Uncertain certainty is a part of any teenager's developmental trajectory and don't doubt or interrogate them about changing their minds about any aspect of their identity; allow for this process and simply reflect that you have noticed their change of views or identity.

6. Support their activism and stance on this matter (so long as it doesn't cross a line into hate speech or prejudice) and

invite them to correct you where you slip up and mislabel them or their friends in this regard, *but* bear in mind that making mistakes can offer valuable learning at many levels because it models that important learning can emerge from mistakes. This is a very important lesson in our 'cancel culture' world where people can be erased online for a transgression or error in judgement.

7. Be curious about your teen's holistic experience. In my work I have met and spoken with many teenagers who feel that every issue, struggle and stress in their life is always brought back to their sexual and gender identity. An LGBTQ+ teenager can still have exam, peer and school stress quite apart from their sexual and gender identity. Stay curious about all of the parts of your teenager's life.

I spoke with a parent of an LGBTQ+ teenager and asked her to share some of her reflections. This is what she told me:

Your daughter identifies as lesbian and has done since middle childhood and she is now a young adult of 19 years old. Looking back, would you share a few of your own reflections on parenting an LGBTQ+ child?

If I'm honest, parenting an LGBTQ+ child is no different from parenting my other children, because she isn't different. She's been the way she is since the day she was born. Maybe that has been my success in parenting her in that the day she told me that she was lesbian, I assured her that absolutely nothing had changed. She was and still is my beautiful daughter. If anything, I was so proud of her for being true to who she is and proud of the bond and relationship that we had that she felt she could tell me.

When did you know that she was gay and what was the realisation like for you? Can you share some of your hopes and worries for her?

I've always had a very open attitude towards my children in that I never gave any thought as to their sexuality. My daughter wrote me an entry in a notebook we shared and it was her first entry where she told me she was gay. I was sitting on the bed in my room. I felt an overwhelming sense of pride and love for her, and I ran to the top of the stairs and called her up and cried as I hugged her. I remember telling her I didn't care what she was, all that mattered was that she was a good person, who followed her heart and was true to herself. I have confidence that my children will follow their own path in life and me spending time worrying about it isn't going to change it. I hope that I've taught them well and that they know, no matter what, the front door is always open and their mum is always here for them. Life is about learning, we all have ups and downs, but it's through those experiences they learn. She's a clever girl with common sense; she always has been, and because of that I knew and still know that she'll be fine.

How have you observed her negotiate the world and develop her sense of self?
Since the day she was born she's had a sense of self which I adore about her. She's very much her own woman, which I admire. She's not afraid to challenge those around her and defend those she feels need defending.

What do you wish you had known or done differently or what learning would you want a parent to know?
The situation with my daughter is a little more complex as we've had to deal with her mental-health issues, which are a separate issue to sexual identity. I think that's an important point. My daughter doesn't have mental-health issues because she's gay; my daughter has mental-health issues and she's gay. The only advice I can give any parent is to empathise with your child, remember what it was like to be their age and to know they haven't changed – this is how they were born and how they have always been. The child you have in front of you is the

exact same child that was in front of you the day before they told you/ you found out they were part of the LGBTQ+ community. Trust in them that they will navigate this themselves and give them the space to do so but ensure they know you're always there for them when/if they need you. Most of all, just enjoy them. My daughter has brought so much joy to my life, and knowing she's being true to herself is the most important thing.

SOCIAL MEDIA – THE ULTIMATE SHAME GAME?

We are parenting teenagers who are growing up and developing while being 'switched on 24/7'. The average teenager will check their social media upwards of 60 times a day and we cannot underestimate the impact on the developing adolescent brain of this level of activity. Teenagers are living their lives, their every waking thought and action, in a very public way on social media, and all of their personal data is being stored on servers owned by large profit-making commercial entities. I am not opposed to the internet; I do believe the pros outweigh the cons and the internet is a very important part of our society. *However,* I do oppose the premature 'adultification' and short-circuiting of development in children, and I believe the consequences for this are far-reaching and impact on all of us.

In June 2017, I delivered a TEDx talk entitled *Social Media – The Ultimate Shame Game?* My question was focused on looking at the relationship of social-media engagement and the propensity to shame and be shamed. I've always been interested in shame and am especially interested in how this plays out online and how this impacts our teenagers and their emotional development during these years.

In that TEDx talk, I recounted being in a secondary school giving a talk about shame and empathy to their 14–15-year-old students. As part of the talk, I had done a version of the activity I have broken down in more detail below under the section entitled 'social media's darker side' whereby I laid out certain social scenarios on flipchart paper around the room and I gave each student a handful of blue and green squares of paper inviting them to walk around and read the various scenarios. If they felt the scenario was okay or socially acceptable to them they would place a green square on the page and if not they would place a blue square on the page. The reason I do this is to establish the baseline I am starting from in terms of how they use and experience social media and what level of shame and shaming is simmering in the group dynamic.

In the instance I referred to in my TEDx talk, I used the scenario of a video of a drunk friend being sexually engaged with someone they wouldn't typically be with going viral and asked if they felt that the sharing of that video was okay or not. I had anticipated an overwhelming NOT OKAY result (my own bias of course) but actually the result was almost exactly 50:50 between those who felt the shaming of their friend was okay (stating she was responsible for her own shaming by virtue of the fact that she had got drunk, did the act and allowed herself to be videoed) and those who felt it wasn't (because she was drunk and not responsible for her actions). Further, many admitted that they would feel justified in sharing that footage too, even if it was someone they knew, 'to teach their friend a lesson'. Others emphasised that they didn't think it was bad to share the footage given it was already online and 'it's not like I took the video and posted it to begin with'.

I don't share this story here to shock you; nor am I seeking to portray these teenagers as a microcosm of what is wrong in society because I do not believe that to be true. I think they offer us a glimpse of what it is like to grow up in a shame society, a generation who cannot say 'before the internet', and have to live with the reality of all of their experiences also existing in a virtual world.

However, I was struck by how quick they were to normalise shame in their lives. Is it a case that shame has become so normalised within our society that we simply take it for granted without acknowledging its presence? I find that to be a scary thought and in wondering how that could have happened, my thoughts drift towards social media.

If you have a social-media account, then you are engaged in shame – I know, an uncomfortable truth for all of us! These virtual places bring out, simultaneously, the very best and worst in us and shine a light on how we can still be a shame society. Look at the myriad of examples of people who have sent a stupid/ ignorant tweet/post or message and, within 24 hours, had their lives 'destroyed' by online vigilantes. There have been some high-profile cases and there are also many more minor cases of someone saying something stupid online and getting lambasted.

As adults, we can easily and almost dismissively say 'just close your social-media accounts and come off it', but that is because we are of a different generation and while social media is pervasive in all of our lives, we have a frame of reference of a before that our teenagers do not have. Add to this that our teenager's very social existence and social engagement with peers is a predominantly online and virtual community. They cannot just come off social media; this is akin to losing their social life as a teenager. Even when they are experiencing cyber-bullying and negative experiences online, they still cannot seem to disengage. It is like having a bruise that you know hurts, but you keep touching it to make sure it still hurts. They compulsively check their social media to see what else people are saying.

While delivering a talk in a secondary school to teenagers (15–17 years old) as part of a youth mental-health programme I was involved in, I invited them to partake in a social experiment. It is worth noting that I delivered this content and same experiment in schools in urban and rural areas, single-sex and mixed school communities, public and private school settings with young people from a variety of socio-economic backgrounds and received the same responses across the board.

I asked for a show of hands in response to these questions:

- How many of you can say that the first thing you do when you wake up is check your social media and the last thing you do before you go to sleep is check your social media = 100 per cent.
- How many of you would say that the only time your mobile phones are powered completely off is when the battery is dead = 100 per cent.
- How many of you would say that you experience some degree of anxiety as a result of your social-media accounts = 100 per cent.
- How many of you would say that knowing it causes you some degree of anxiety would encourage you to close your social-media accounts = 0 per cent.
- How many of you would be prepared to power your mobile phones totally off at 8 p.m. every night and not turn them back on before 8 a.m. the next morning every night for ten consecutive nights = 10 per cent.

Yes, just 10 per cent were prepared to try my experiment. Interestingly, the others told me they were just being honest, as they didn't want to lie to me when they knew they wouldn't do it.

I followed up with the 10 per cent and the findings were also interesting. Eight per cent completed all ten days and of those who did they reported:

- improved quality of sleep
- feeling calmer and more rested in general
- increased focus on school work

- more positive relationships with family members, especially parents
- lower levels of anxiety and worry.

But when I asked if they would be prepared to keep it up, not even these benefits would convince them to do so. They all also reported feeling that they had missed out on 'stuff' with their peers as a result of the phones being switched off. They said that they were playing catch-up on things that had happened with friends (often drama-related such as rows or mean comments but also funny and interesting material). This told me that they are constantly connected, albeit in a virtual way, and never get that downtime, that break from each other that we all need to process and assimilate the events of our days, to reflect and think about conversations and things that might have happened during the day. I had asked for 12 hours of no phone or social-media contact at a time when ideally they should be winding down and sleeping and they felt that they missed too much during this time.

(RE)EXPANDING EMPATHY

So how is it a case that a generation of teenagers who are constantly in contact can seemingly show so little empathy for a friend when distressing material goes viral and openly admit that they may even participate in their friend's shame? Is it a case of lower levels of empathy perhaps?

What is the difference between saying something online and to someone's face? I believe it is twofold: first, the degree of empathy that gets lost online and second, the fact that when you say something online about someone, it doesn't feel like you are saying it *to* them, it doesn't feel real and therefore the potential consequences are not considered. It has become so easy to interact virtually that we are investing less and less time engaging with people at a personal level and this is having a profound effect on our empathy levels.

The University of Michigan (2010)[11] measured the empathy levels in college students and compared them to previous generations at the same age (14,000 students over a 30-year period) and found that over the course of their study, the groups of young people started to show significantly lower levels of empathy towards others than previous generations, with the biggest drop being after 2010 when empathy levels measured up to 40 per cent lower than their counterparts 30 years previously. This period marks the birth and rise of social media and young children/teens having smartphones with constant internet access. I am not inferring causation but it's an interesting correlation here.

Children develop empathy skills at approximately three years of age onwards (though the capacity is building from infancy) through projective play (see Appendix A), when we see an increase in narrative-based play to re-enact real-life events as a means of better understanding them. Engaging in this kind of play forces children to consider the perspectives of others and thereby develops empathy, capacity for critical thinking and the capacity for problem-solving, all of which are developmentally essential and help to build our social intelligence levels, enabling us to read potentially dangerous situations and also develop and sustain relationships. What we are seeing now is a generation who have not successfully negotiated this stage, likely because of an increased focus on virtual play and virtual interaction with people who are not a physical part of their real world. Screen-based play and virtual engagement on digital devices *can* be fun and pose no real threat to the psychosocial development of children and young people so long as it is *a part* of our children's lives and not the main thrust of how they play and/or interact and connect with others. A screen can supplement connection when in-person connection is not possible (as is the case for parents and children who live very far apart from each other or with friends or family members who have moved away), but it can never fully be a substitute for it. As my own child said to me recently, 'I like seeing Nanny and Grandad on the phone but I like feeling their hugs more.' We need relational, intersubjective, in-person, face-to-face contact with each other to feel and sustain a connection. It is *this* kind of connection that allows us to grow and develop, and a screen cannot achieve this.

Modern parenting is totally different from ever before and it's important that parents feel supported in this journey. Parents have to become familiar with a whole new and ever-evolving technological world while keeping lines of communication open from the youngest ages to ensure that theirs is the message that teenagers default to when it comes to making choices and taking risks.

SOCIAL MEDIA'S DARKER SIDE

Most teenagers say that social media helps them to feel better connected to their peers and to better understand their emotions, and yet the vast majority also say that drama online is a cause of tension and anxiety and that drama is an ongoing part of their social-media interaction with their peers. I do want to preface this by saying that I believe that there are a myriad of pro-social benefits to social media, and the dark side does not cancel those benefits out. That being said, the dark side is truly dark and the ramifications are far-reaching. What I would like to do is look at some of the dominant negative experiences teenagers have online, such as cyber-bullying and social shaming and also explore this question: why do so many teenagers turn away from the adults in their lives and towards the internet/social media for relationships?

Cyber-bullying is one such consequence of the darker side of social media. Cyber-bullying is very serious and often leads to significant psychosocial problems like depression, isolation, loneliness, stress, anxiety, low self-esteem and, in extreme situations, self-harm and even suicidal thoughts/actions. It is serious and deserves to be taken seriously. It is also not, by any means, an exclusively teenage phenomenon. Plenty of adults engage in cyber-bullying or are cyber-bullied. Plenty of websites exist aimed at an adult demographic with the sole purpose of sharing gossip or nasty comments about others. Before you seek to address online behaviour and issues around cyber-bullying with your teenager, take time to reflect on your own behaviour online and the way you use and engage with it.

I speak about this topic a lot with teenagers and the main hurdle I find is that they can be very unforgiving online, in a way they are not in the real world. They feel that if a person posts something, it becomes fair game to comment on it in any way they like. They have very different understandings as to what constitutes 'abuse' online than perhaps we adults do. So it is always worth starting from a place of wondering to establish a baseline for how they behave and expect others to behave online.

15-MINUTE ACTIVITY

I do a version of this activity at my school talks whereby I write certain social scenarios onto flip-chart paper and leave them lying around the room and I give everyone some blue squares and green squares of paper, telling them that they should place a green square on the scenario if they deem it acceptable behaviour or a blue square if they don't. The results are eye-opening to say the least. So try a modified version of this to get a snapshot of how your teenager might view or respond to things online based on what they believe is acceptable.

- Give them the different-coloured squares or just two different markers.
- Write out three to five social-media-based scenarios on A4 sheets of paper and lie them on the table. Use something like, but not exactly, these examples, as yours should resonate with your teenager and also your own questions/wonderings.
  - A friend is drunk at a party and is hooking up with someone you know they wouldn't hook up with if they were sober. No one steps in to take them aside but another friend makes a video of the hook-up. The video gets posted online and shared all around school and beyond.
  - Someone you follow on your social media posts a selfie of themselves on a night out with friends. People are commenting that they look awful and asking if they might be unwell.
  - You receive a screenshot showing a recent social-media post of someone you know. Another friend has sent it to you and a few others on a group message with an eye-roll and vomit emoji underneath. You each forward it to at least two others with similar sentiments.
  - You gave your friend your passwords while you were away (to maintain your snapchat streaks and keep an eye on your ex) and recently discovered that someone has been 'liking' posts and leaving emojis under pictures on your behalf. You know that it must be your friend as no one else has your passwords. They strongly deny it.
  - You left your phone behind and unlocked while you went to the shop with your friend. Your parent checked your social-media accounts

while you were gone but you only know this
because they have been asking about things
they couldn't otherwise know about.

- Put one or other colour on these yourself and if
  anyone else is around (other teens/adults) they can
  do it too.
- The important part is that you do not judge what
  your teenager has put down. This isn't about right/
  wrong; it is about deepening your insight and
  understanding into how they see the world.
- After you have had a chance to look at the
  reactions that each scenario elicited, sit together
  and talk about your views, where they converge/
  diverge, what the story is that you each tell yourselves
  when you look at these scenarios, and how would
  you feel if it was you – would that change how you
  feel about the answers? Wonder if anything like this
  has ever happened for real and what that story is.

I would always include something about sharing passwords
because while trust between parents and teenagers can be a fragile
tightrope to walk at times, they tend to bestow their closest friends
with limitless trust, supremely confident that Best Friends Forever
is a fact not a cute bear motif. A breach in friendship trust can be
akin to the effect of a relationship heartbreak and its impact is not
to be dismissed or taken lightly. But because of this limitless trust
in each other, when a friendship goes sour (and they do sometimes)
the betrayal can be huge and the personal information that was
shared can have significant social consequences for your teenager.
Talk with them about trust and boundaries and how a trusting
relationship is not one without personal boundaries.

Teenagers (like many adults, to be honest) feel empowered or at least disinhibited enough to 'say' things online in a post or a text to/about someone that they might never say to that person if it were a real-life/person-to-person conversation they were having. It has never been easier to be cruel and nasty and what might be a micro-aggression in real life that could simmer and get worked out without blowing up will become amplified very quickly online. You might have seen particular (adult) talk shows that have celebrities sit and read aloud some of the nasty comments strangers have said about them online. This is not something we give enough consideration to. With the advance of social media, the celebrities who once seemed so far out of reach are suddenly just a tag away and it can be easy to objectify them as some 'thing' and forget that they are people. Once we can do that about celebrities, it's not such a leap to start doing it about the people in our lives too, until it doesn't feel real if it didn't happen in the real world. But what is said online is real, about real people and has real consequences. We must get this across to our teenagers now if we want to bring about a meaningful change to the online environment, which can quickly descend into startling toxicity.

15-MINUTE ACTIVITY

- Write out examples of nasty messages/texts – these can be ones you have seen/received/sent (there is no end to examples online – we have all seen them) or even made up to suit the situation or your teenager.
  - ° Include direct nasty comments (body comments are common).
  - ° Include ones that are a positive dressed up as a negative, for example: *You're pretty; you would be even prettier if you lost some weight <heart emoji>*.

- ° Include ones that are *about* a person rather than *to* them, for example: *@someone else, did you see this, lol, the state of it.*
- ° Include some that are presented as a comment about the person whose post it is but are actually a way of making it about yourself, for example: *Actually can't cope with how unreal you are. I'm such a loser when I look at you. You are actual goals but I know I could never match up <crying face emoji/broken heart emoji>.*

- I like to mix in a few funnier ones or ones that could be interpreted either way, as the funny ones provide some playful light relief and the ones that could be interpreted either way stimulate active reflection and discussion while encouraging more perspective-taking to hear that others might hear it differently from how they do.
- Now sit opposite each other and say these messages directly to each other, using a tone of voice, facial expression and body language that is congruent with what you read. You want to focus on saying it as you would in a conversation with someone more than simply reading it from a piece of paper.
- Reflect on how it feels:
  - ° to say it
  - ° to hear it
  - ° to see how the other person is receiving it.
  Reflect on why someone would feel it is okay to write this online when it is definitely not comfortable or okay to say it in real life.

- If your teenager is telling you that it feels okay to say it (it really shouldn't, as you should ensure you are including some ones that are *definitely* over any kind of acceptable line), consider that this is bravado and emphasise that it has really upset you even though it's just an activity you are doing together. Wonder what must it be like if it happened for real and how awful it must be to open up your social-media accounts and read such things.
- Wonder if they have any real-life experience of this happening – start by 'othering' it and wonder about it having happened to their friends before you do so about them.

Given that adolescence is a time of self-development and deepening one's awareness of how others experience and feel about you, social media has pros and cons. When your teenager posts something, they get feedback as to how their peers see them in the form of likes, shares, comments and so on. This gives them a tangible read as to how their thoughts, feelings and actions about something affect or make an impression on others. However, this can lead to a herd-mentality thought process whereby they post for the purpose of eliciting this validation without it being authentically them or reflective of who they are. This does not nurture an authentic sense of self – quite the opposite – and can in fact bring anxiety, low mood (even depression) and uncertainty instead. Adolescents, developmentally, seek out affirmation and validation from others, but the easy and constant access to an abundant stream of feedback can create a loop of constantly seeking/needing this validation and not feeling 'good enough' without it. Combining this tidal wave of feedback with a teenager's (developmental) lack of critical thinking can lead to them identifying as depressed when actually they are feeling upset, demoralised, disappointed or even distressed. This *can* result in teenagers confusing the clinical term 'depression' with what are unpleasant but commonplace negative emotions.

Also consider how social media can so easily result in the formation of echo chambers because we frequently follow accounts of people who think like we do and thus not only don't challenge but actually reinforce our own world view on things. Social media can certainly fuel or motivate greater participation in society/ community and even inspire actions that aim to make a positive difference in the lives of others, but it also serves to drive narcissism and feeding off each other's obsessions and fixations. So while it can be a mirror for their emerging sense of self, it can also be a façade that results in teenagers growing up with more anxiety and less self-esteem. This is why parents do need to be engaged with their teenagers' engagement with social media – this does not mean spying on them or checking up by following them from a fake account *but* rather engaging with them through conversation, reflective activities, playful and connected chats in an open and ongoing way as opposed to waiting for it to become a problem. This way, they are more likely to come to you when or if it does become a problem.

When it comes to parenting versus social media, it is a battle we will not win if we approach it through confrontation. How we will beat it is if we can approach it with and through the lens of relational communication. We want to raise kind, empathic, reflective and considerate independent young adults who can live *with* rather than *through* social media. Use its pro-social benefits of connectivity and community but ensure it is not your or your teenager's *only* source of connectivity and community. Ensure that you are making time and creating space for some kind of relational connection with your teenager each day. Ideas include:

- A 15-minute chat about their day/your day.
- A 15-minute chat about a podcast/TV show you both watch (even if you only watch or listen to it so that you can have this moment of meeting with them).
- A 15-minute 'wondering' chat about something topical on the news/social media.
- A 15-minute playful activity (nurture when soothing and reassurance are needed and something engagement based when it's fun and a laughter release is needed).

Whatever you do, make a 15-minute connection your parental goal each day with your teenager. Believe me, it is a small change that will make a big difference.

DISCERNING AND DISARMING DISCRIMINATION

So much discrimination and marginalisation lingers in our world, and our teenagers are so skilled in standing up to and calling this out. This doesn't mean that they are always right or that the way they go about this is perfect, but does that apply to any of us, regardless of age? I think not. We are always and forever in a state of learning, and this means making mistakes and learning from them as we continue to evolve in our thinking and understanding about things.

Teenagers make great activists because they are believers – they want to change the world and believe that they can, and they are brave and passionate people. There are many examples of teenagers whose activism has and is changing our world for the better (Greta Thunberg, Isra Hirsi and Jamie Margolin, all campaigning for climate change action; Malala Yousafzai campaigning for educational rights; the Parkland shooting survivors, campaigning for better gun control; Marley Dias, campaigning for diversity in representation and founder of the #1000BlackGirlBooks; Riya Goel and Vanessa Louis-Jean, campaigning for racial equality and justice; Salomé Beyer, campaigning against gender-based violence; Mari Copeny, whose letter to then President Obama at just eight years old brought the water crisis in Flint Michigan into the spotlight and who continues to campaign for better water quality for all; and Desmond Napoles (also known as Desmond Is Amazing), campaigning for LGBTQ+ youth visibility to name but a small few).

How to activate your activist

I am constantly impressed and inspired by the teenagers that I have had the privilege to work with. We should always encourage our teenagers to use their voice and bring their passion to the frontline of the issues that matter to them, that matter to all of us. Encourage your teenager to find a cause that they are passionate about and then support their activism in that area, even if/when it is a topic that might not resonate with you or align with your personal views on the topic.

I was sitting in a café one day (I am a devoted people-watcher; you might say eavesdropper, and that might be fair too) and there was a father and teenage daughter sitting just behind me so I could hear their conversation clearly. It started when the dad returned from the counter with their drinks and the teenage girl had been scrolling on her phone while he was away. The conversation went like this:

Dad: On your phone, mindlessly scrolling social media again. What's wrong with just sitting with your thoughts?

Daughter: I don't just 'sit with my thoughts', Dad; I do something with them. You should try it.

Dad: Oh really, and what can you do with your thoughts on your phone in the few minutes I was gone?

Daughter: As it happens, I was confirming shared transport for some friends and me to travel into the city to attend a protest rally to fight for equality for asylum seekers coming into this country. I was sending a message to the minibus company and then a message to the campaign group to give them the details and yes, that just takes a few minutes and a phone.

Dad: What? Who are this group? How long have you been involved in this? Is it safe for you to go? Does your mother know about this?
    <A deep sigh and a lengthy pause. I like to think she was taking her time to both decide how she would respond and allow him to hear his own barrage of doubts and questions.>

Daughter: One of the group has had to drop out so there's a spare seat on the bus if you want to come too.

Dad: Honey, this issue is more complex than it might seem.

Daughter: I know, Dad, but the solution is simpler than it's being made out to be.

She went on to speak with insight, passion and yes a healthy sprinkle of idealism too, but that's not such a bad thing.
    I'd like to think that he took that spare seat on the minibus and went with her, and as I had to leave before they got that far, I'm choosing to believe that he did.

I was once delivering a parent talk in a community centre when a parent raised their hand and asked a question about having discovered internet searches on a shared home computer that alerted her that her teen was engaged in political lobbying on an issue that she was personally opposed to. It was about veganism and the dairy farming industry. She was asking me what she should do about it. Having sat and reflected on her own views and feelings aloud, I wondered if her teenager's views could change her mind about how she felt. She vehemently said 'absolutely not' so I wondered why she thought she could change his mind with her views. Instead, she decided to raise the issue with him and to help him link in with organisations that could provide him with information and buy him a vegan cookbook so that he could pursue veganism at home.

Civic participation and activism is a great outlet for teenagers because it is pro-social, an outlet for frustration and anger, and supports social engagement and belief formation. It supports their emerging identity and the development of more autonomy from their parents, while also giving them group inclusion experience and skills around working collaboratively with like-minded individuals. Given that this is also a time for testing and resisting authority, challenging the status quo and pushing boundaries, activism can be a positive way of channelling this energy for them. It is empowering to be encouraged to use your voice, and activism is a healthy way of expressing passionate thoughts and deepening awareness and understanding of the world outside themselves.

CHAPTER 8

The Darker Side of Adolescence (Extreme Behaviours)

A lot of what I have written about in this book so far is about what represents normal, healthy, albeit at times very challenging and even unpleasant, adolescent development. In part this is because I believe that it is important to get a baseline for what is normal adolescent development before we psychopathologise (see everything as a behavioural dysfunction or a psychological problem) what may certainly be difficult and challenging without being atypical development.

So how do you know when your struggle in parenting your teenager or their struggle in negotiating adolescence is above and beyond what is normal? It is usually when *everything* you are trying (in line with what has come so far in this book) is just not working, but it will also be when you see a pervasive negativity that is affecting all areas of your life and your teenager's life. It will also be when you don't have a specific context within which you can locate and make sense of the behaviour you are seeing and when the potential consequences for the behaviour in question are at the extreme end. Let me break some of these areas down a little further now for you to make better sense of this.

MENTAL ILLNESS

I have talked about the difference between mental health, mental well-being and mental illness in Chapter 4, where we took a closer look at the prevalence of anxiety in adolescence. The World Health Organisation cites that worldwide 10–20 per cent of children and adolescents will experience a mental disorder and that as high as half of all mental illnesses begin by the age of 14 years old and three-quarters by mid-twenties. This is prime brain development time and while environmental factors tend to play a hugely significant role in adolescents' mental health and mental well-being, the neurobiological aspect of mental illness is very activated in this phase of development too.

While the majority of teenagers will negotiate the ups and downs of adolescence relatively smoothly and relatively unscathed (some level of mild struggle is entirely healthy and normal, after all) and gradually move away from dependence on their parents/caregivers and towards more independent and self-sufficient adult living, some teenagers will really struggle, and in profound ways, as they stumble their way through adolescence. In adolescence, we see a sharp rise in the incidence of psychiatric mental illnesses, most notably anxiety/mood disorders, psychosis, eating disorders, personality disorders and significant substance abuse and its associated impact on mind and body. Increasingly, some research is exploring these disorders emerging as a consequence of anomalous brain changes during the phase of adolescent brain development.

We know that strengthening and enhancing our children's social skills, problem-solving skills, investing in empathy and self-esteem and gradually extending their self-efficacy and self-confidence can help prevent mental-health problems emerging in late childhood/early adolescence. These include (but are not limited to) conditions such as conduct disorders, anxiety, depression and eating disorders as well as other negative risk-taking behaviours, including those that relate to harmful sexual behaviour, alcohol/substance abuse and aggressive or even violent behaviour.

This is precisely why I have written this series of 15-Minute Parenting books. The best defence we have against psychopathology emerging in children and young people is to invest in our parenting. Playing, inviting play and being playful in how we connect and communicate with and nurture our children's growth and development is an investment in their mental health. It doesn't mean that nothing will go wrong or awry in adolescence, but it means that you already have a road map to support you in a connected way in parenting through whatever comes up. This certainly doesn't mean you and you alone should have all of the answers – you couldn't possibly nor should you attempt to assume a position of all-knowing. Knowing when to reach out to bring in a professional who can ensure that you and your teenager are best supported is an active part of connected parenting.

Mental health is about happiness, connection, a sense of belonging and acceptance and being actively engaged in one's social network (school/peers/hobbies/family). Signs that your teen's mental health is in trouble are sudden and otherwise unexplained changes to the above and general mood disruption. Signs of mental illness are when these changes increase, have a pervasive impact on their capacity to function and are a constant (or very regular) presence regardless of environmental variables. We want to parent in a way that safeguards and nurtures our teenager's mental health, actively supports them through the challenges to their mental health and that empowers us to act quickly in seeking professional intervention when we see signs of mental illness emerging.

Staying positive and using mindfulness and meditation-style activities are very helpful in nurturing our mental health and in staying mentally healthy. However, positivity alone cannot effect change or meet the needs of someone whose mental health is negatively compromised or is showing signs of mental illness. This requires prompt and appropriate referral to suitably trained and qualified mental-health professionals. I really do want to be clear about this point.

And because I do think positive thinking and positive reframing of situations can be effective self-regulation tools, I want to share one that I use myself and have always found a really healthy and self-nurturing tool. First, I will talk you through how to use it for your parent-self and then how to (only slightly) adapt it as something you can do with your teenagers so that they can go on to do it daily/regularly for themselves. This should not be treated as an exercise to try to do *only* when you are experiencing negative thoughts/feelings but more as something you can integrate into your daily activities, perhaps as you wind down in the evenings.

15-MINUTE POSITIVE-THINKING EXERCISE

This is a great reflective practice to develop so that you can acquire a deeper capacity to think more positively about the aspects of your life/your day/your relationship that have gone well and why this is. It will also strengthen and enhance your capacity to positively reframe a day that maybe hasn't gone so well by spotlighting its most positive part. People who have developed a capacity to think positively do not ignore or overlook the negative and more challenging aspects of their lives – far from it. But they can better extract the good and seek to amplify the positive parts of their lives while holding an innate belief that things can, often are and will be better than those darker moments. When people do this activity every day (or certainly most days in the week) for 15 consecutive days they report feeling happier, less prone to ruminating on negative things, lower levels of worry and/or sadness and describe themselves as calmer and less likely to snap or lose their tempers with others. Treat yourself (and your teenager when bringing this to them) to a fancy new journal/notebook.

1. Each day for the 15 days, give yourself 15 minutes before you go to sleep to write down three things

that went well and why. This could be something
as simple as 'My son smiled at me this morning'.
Or it might be a major event such as 'I was
offered a new job today'.

2. Underneath each thing that went well, write what
   you did to make it happen. For example, if you
   put 'My son smiled at me today', you could write
   'I caught his eye for a few seconds and smiled at
   him and noticed that he saw me see him and he
   smiled back'.

3. It might take some time to think of things to write
   down at first, but the more regularly you do it,
   the more fluent you become with it. Try to give
   it a go for 15 days but start even smaller if that
   is overwhelming and say that you will do it for a
   week. However many days you remember to do
   it, you are building a collection of these moments
   to read back on any time you need a reminder,
   which I find especially helpful on one of those
   particularly challenging days.

Bring this exercise to your teenager

It might be helpful if you can start by doing this exercise with your
teenager to begin with. They may not understand what you mean
or why it would be helpful and you want this to be presented in a
way that avoids it feeling like an assignment but is experienced as
a fun and worthwhile thing to do. Perhaps share with them that
you do this and would love to share your notes at the end of the
week or invite them to pick one day's positivity to swap with you.
This is about helping your teenager to think about things that have
gone well for them and then to reflect on why this went well, what

other variables contributed to the successful outcome. Identifying this pattern empowers your teenager to do more of those things that result in successful outcomes/things going well for them. It is also helpful in supporting them to identify opposing patterns that may contribute to those things that do not go well, however this part should be viewed as a secondary gain from this process while the primary focus is the positivity tracking.

I am highlighting this as something to do with your teenagers but actually you could also start this with your younger children and keep it going as they grow up. It is never too early to start this, but it is also never too late to begin it. A younger child might note how pleased they are about a picture they drew or a play date they had. An older child/teenager might note an exam that went well, a match that they won, a difficult conversation that went better than they had anticipated. There is no right or wrong with this. Never judge or assess the positive thing that is noted. Never wonder aloud *was this really the best part of your day?* This is about developing a mental-health investment practice and all positive experiences are valid.

If you would like to take this a step further you can get a cork noticeboard, some paper, scissors and board pins and make a positivity collage of the previous month's highlights that can hang up in their bedroom so that they can see it all the time or hang it on the inside of a wardrobe door so that they see it some of the time/as needed.

DARK THEMES IN ADOLESCENT MULTIMEDIA

Darkness is thematic in adolescence, not just in terms of their development but also in their external worlds. All you have to do is look to themes of books, TV and movies directed at the teenage audience to see evidence of this. The occult, vampires, drugs, sex and murder dominate. Teenagers are often handling very adult material alone and away from the barely present parental figures in these shows. Are themes in teenage dramas becoming darker as a direct response to the struggles of teenagers today *or* are these themes contributing to how teenagers believe their lives should look and feel today? Personally, I think dark themes have dominated children's books since *Grimm's Fairy Tales* and that generally speaking dark themes help young people to make sense of the darkness in life rather than cause it. The hyper-sexualisation we tend to see with adult actors portraying teenagers with unrealistic body types and flawless complexions might be more problematic and we do need to gently yet firmly challenge these *unrealities*.

Research is available but can appear contradictory in this area. For example, there is research to show that teenagers are extremely impressionable when engaged with multimedia[12] and this research showed a consistent relationship between being exposed to sexual content in the media and adolescent attitudes towards sex and sexual behaviour. This 2008 research highlighted that when adolescents don't have experiences in real life to refer to, they normalise what they see represented in the media as something that is supposed to happen or is expected of them. I have heard this in my adolescent clinic when teenage girls are telling me that all body hair is disgusting because they rarely see it represented on screen. Equally, teenage boys have sat opposite me talking about how much protein and supplements and home weight-based workouts they are doing so that their bodies measure up to what they see represented as the teenage male body (actually adult actors with a particular adult physique playing teenagers) ideal on screen. So anecdotally, I have seen some impact in my work.

Teenager's response (16-year-old girl)

I think some aspects of the darker themes in our TV shows heavily influence teenagers. Take, for example, the body types in these shows. How do you think it feels to see grown adults playing 16-year-olds? They have fully grown and developed bodies that we compare to our own still-developing bodies. I think that's a huge problem with teen drama shows. Not only do these shows cast six-foot men to play teenage boys and D-cup and size 6 (UK) women to play girls but they also imply that serious relationships are the norm for every single teenager. While this may well be the norm for some teenagers, it's actually perfectly normal and common not to have a boyfriend or girlfriend and is definitely normal not to have one that you're constantly having sex with!

Some teen dramas show dark themes beyond just sexy 'teens' having loads of sex and some of those can be helpful in highlighting stuff that you feel you might be the only one experiencing and can get a conversation going on tricky stuff. But personally, I've seen a number of shows that normalise self-harm and that can be really worrying because it might delay someone reaching out for help or it risks telling them that it's normal to cut or hurt yourself when it's not – it's a sign that you need help. As teenagers, we can experience a range of very strong emotions, some of which are really hard to deal with or even to speak about, so if we see someone on a TV show who seemingly has the same feelings or struggles as us we can more easily identify with them and feel less alone in those feelings, like we're not the only ones who feel this way. If we then see them using self-harm as a way of coping it can imply that this is a way that might help us to deal with what's happening, so we might also try it.

Across the body of research in this area, evidence that such exposure causes long-term harmful effects is inconclusive at best. For example, in the USA, the Centres for Disease Control and Prevention conduct research[13] every two years into youth risk behaviour with millions of teenagers and found that teenagers are very unlikely to engage in any of the behaviours they see in teen dramas.

Teenager's response (17-year-old boy)

Yeah, teenagers know that what we see on TV shows is massively exaggerated of course. When a teen's sex life is really wild and they're having a lot of sex, it does come across as unrealistic. Sex is normal and teenagers definitely have sex, but when it's at this crazy amount of sex level it's unrealistic but also makes me pause and question if I should be having more sex and more of this type of wild sex than I am. In this way, I think that TV shows do add to the pressure of teenagers feeling that they need to have sex by a certain age rather than waiting until they're truly ready for it. It can make us feel like we're not 'normal' when most of these so-called teenage characters seem really ready and happy to do it all of the time. It's similar with body image for me and, I know, other guys as well. I feel that many of the characters on teen TV shows don't really depict a normal teenage body because very attractive adults who don't even look like teenagers to be honest play them all. That said, sometimes I do find myself saying, 'Gosh, is that how I'm supposed to look?' and I worry that people wouldn't find me attractive if I don't measure up to these characters. So it's a mix of knowing it's not realistic or representative yet also questioning if my life would feel better if it was more like what I see.

What is clear is that this issue is nuanced and the degree of influence these themes in TV shows has over teenagers is heavily influenced by other life variables such as if they are already sexually active or not, if they live in a family where such themes are openly discussed and gently yet firmly challenged or not, attitudes to alcohol, drugs and risk at home, and so on.

It is undeniable that TV for teenagers has become much darker in the last ten years, but there's also a situation where teen dramas are being watched by adults, so my inference is that many of the themes in these shows are intended to engage and hold an adult audience as well as a teen one in an attempt to bridge the adolescent and adult markets.

There's something in the make-up of a teenager's brain that responds particularly well to the tropes in these shows because developmentally, the teenage brain is being rewired, and they're moving towards risk-taking and impulsive behaviours, and that will compel and lure teenagers towards high-adrenaline, high-drama shows. Further, if you watch any of these shows (and if you haven't I strongly suggest that you do consider *Pretty Little Liars, Riverdale, 13 Reasons Why, Skins, Euphoria*, among others), you'll often find that the pace is pretty hectic, with no real space to assimilate each plot. It's sort of like information overdosing. Given that the teenagers' default position is often that of drama and, you'll know this from living with and parenting them, it can be calm, then a full-on tantrum, then back to calm, the trends of these dark teen TV shows feed right into that (dys)regulatory rollercoaster of emotion, and it is often this pattern that draws our teenagers into these dramas rather than the actual content in the scenes.

The real issue and answer is not about censoring material in TV shows, movies or books. There is darkness in life and it is actually really important that these themes can be explored in this way. The real issue lies in creating and maintaining open and honest conversation within the parent–teen connection and working towards media literacy in our young people to ensure that they can more easily identify what is real and fake and what is fantasy and reality with a critical, analytical and reflective mind.

While we know, for instance, that these shows contain actors in their twenties playing teenagers, this may not necessarily be apparent to a teenager. Further, I would argue that the problem isn't with the specific content in the scenes, it's when this stuff is accepted as normal teenage behaviour. That being said, don't ban a TV show that you have heard a lot of negative press about but rather use it as a way to broach such burning topics that can be awkward and difficult to bring up without a reference.

Your teenagers will see this material whether you want them to or not, so seek to insert yourself into the world of your teenager. Be curious and interested but not intrusive, which can be a fine line to tread. Sit with them, or watch it yourself, and be prepared to be shocked. Say to your child, 'That was a lot for me; can we talk about what that was about? It would really help me to talk this through.' They may dismiss your concerns and say some of it was normal and standard, but they will also reassure you that much of it was overstated, exaggerated and unrealistic. You may even be able to have a laugh at how ridiculous some of it was.

I really think that we have to give teenagers more credit than they usually get. The makers of these so-called teen dramas need to remember that teenagers don't need to see every detail spelled out to understand what's going on. To do so is really disrespectful to a teenager's intelligence.

SELF-HARM

Not much else will trigger the kind of panic and anxiety in a parent than discovering that your teenager has been self-injuring. Unfortunately, it is actually quite common in this age group and the causes or motivations vary widely. Marking the skin with cuts, scratches and burns, picking or biting the skin or hitting one's own body until it bruises are the most common forms of self-injury.

Teens with a diagnosis of anxiety, depression, eating disorders or who may have experienced trauma are all at risk for self-harm, but so are young people with a history of any of the following:

- low self-esteem
- feeling rejected or lonely
- feeling unsafe at school or at home
- pervasive perfectionism
- frequent conflicts with friends or family
- impulsive behaviour
- a tendency to take unhealthy risks (behaviours that could result in physical harm).

Often this behaviour has been going on for a long time before a parent might discover it. It is far from being the *attention-seeking behaviour* it is often mistakenly described as, since teenagers who engage in self-injury are very good at concealing it from others, and while you might see some scars or marks, the signs of self-injury are often much more subtle than this. Always be mindful of any sudden, significant and unexplained (no specific context such as a bereavement or parental separation, etc.) behaviour change and look out for any of the following:

- suspicious-looking scars
- wounds that don't heal or get worse over time
- isolation from peers/family or spending increased amount of time alone in bedroom
- talking about self-injury (they might mention peers who engage in self-harm)
- keeping sharp items in their bedroom that would typically be in a shared space (razors, scissors, a sharp shard of glass/porcelain)

- secretive behaviour – beyond what is typical and healthy
- wearing long sleeves and/or long trousers in hot weather
- avoiding social activities as a pattern
- wearing a lot of bandages or wrapping hairbands or scarves around forearms
- avoiding sports or other activities where they might have to change clothes in front of others.

None of these in and of themselves is an indicator of self-harming behaviour, but what you should look out for is a sudden and unexplained shift in any of these or a number of these areas. If this is familiar, do not approach your teenager with an *aha, I've got you* style of approach but do so with curiosity and empathy, staying in that all-important inquisitive stance of not-knowing and seeking to better understand. Your response in the moment matters and your reaction thereafter matters.

You may feel a range of feelings in the face of learning about your teen's self-harming behaviour and you may well feel these in a rush, very quickly. You might feel fear, anxiety, shock, sadness and even anger. You may feel pulled towards the *How could you do this to yourself* and *You HAVE to stop this now!* This is all perfectly normal and understandable, and it's not as if you have a script for these moments, *but* honestly, even if you did have a script, it won't be what comes to your mind in the moment of discovery. Why not? Because when you discover something that strikes you to your very core, your reaction comes from a more primitive place. Your own attachment system is activated and you (emotionally) flip your lid with your limbic area firing all of those fight/flight/freeze signals to you. In *this* state you cannot reach for that script, you simply react in a raw and real way and that is not always the 'right response' but it is the real response. It is afterwards when you have had time, space and distance to self-regulate that you find the words to say what you wished you had said or the invitation to hug that you wished you had opened with. It is never too late to do or say the right thing. In this emotionally dysregulated state, it is all too easy to say the wrong thing or to say something in the wrong way because you are speaking from your emotional centre and not the logical, reasoning part of your brain. I find it helpful to have some 'stock statements' that serve as a holding response while I internally grapple to bring my own thoughts and feelings back in line. Try to use 'I' statements that honour your authentic feelings on the subject but don't drag you into a conversation you are not yet ready to have. I might use something like:

- *Wow, that's a lot for me to try to process in this moment. I'll take some time to sit with this and I would be happy to talk about it later/at X time.*
- *I'm feeling a lot of emotion in response to what's been said/ what's happened. I don't want to speak from this place and I need time to be able to think clearer about this.*
- *Thank you for telling me this. I understand how difficult it must have been and I see how brave you are. I want to be able to respond as best I can and I cannot do that in this moment so let's take some space from each other and have a chat about it later when we've both had some time.*
- *I don't know what to say because I'm feeling so much right now. I need to feel these feelings before I can make sense of it all. I hope you understand that.*
- *I feel that if I say anything right now it will be the wrong thing. I believe the right thing is that I walk away and have a cry and get some clarity. I love you. We'll talk about this later.*

You can always go back and own what happened in an open and honest way: *'I didn't say or do what I wished I had when I learned about this. I think that's because I felt so scared about what it meant and so sad that I didn't know this before now and couldn't help you.*

I'm so sorry. Can I try again now, because there is something else I would like to say or do now that I think is more about you and how you might be feeling than is about my feelings and me.' Our children and teenagers are very forgiving of our transgressions – they will give us a second chance, so always ask for one when you need it.

It is helpful to bear in mind that just as this is scary for you, it is also really scary for your teenager. They might be holding some blend of guilt, shame, fear, regret and deep sadness of their own. You have to find a way to stay open and out of judgement on this (as with so much else). Be there to listen, truly listen, and think and feel it through together.

Offer reassurance that you will talk to some people and find someone who can help. Be very clear that this is not something that you can keep secret because it needs help from professionals who understand this issue better than you can. Reach out to your GP, who will be able to refer you to child and adolescent mental-health services and/or a private adolescent psychotherapist with experience in this area. See if there are any services (often run by the not-for-profit sector) in your area which can offer immediate crisis counselling sessions for self-injury/suicidal ideation as a holding space while you wait for an appointment with other services.

Teenager's story (14-year-old girl)

Honestly, I just remember being relieved when my parents found out about my cutting. It freaked me out that I did it and yet I couldn't stop doing it. It started by accident really. I was feeling really anxious and upset, and my parents kept asking me what was wrong, but the truth was I really didn't know so I kept shrugging and saying nothing. I could see that this made them frustrated with me and that just made my anxiety worse. I accidentally cut myself in the bathroom while I was shaving my legs and I remember just staring at the blood as it poured down my leg. The cut was actually quite deep so there was a lot of blood and I knew it hurt, but I also felt relief and I started to cry and cry like I hadn't since I was a kid.

My mother came in and was so worried and took care of the cut. She thought that this was why I was crying so I said that it was. I felt so calm afterwards. For a while anyway. And the next time I felt my anxiety building, I cut my leg with the blade from my razor and it just kept going from there. I was only found out because I'd forgotten to lock the bathroom door and my dad walked in and saw me while I was doing it. I've never seen him look like that before. He froze, went pale and looked like he might vomit or cry all at once. There was some shouting then and my mother did cry and I don't think any of us slept too well that first night, but the next day we sat together and made a plan. There were more tears but there were also hugs. It hasn't been easy but it is easier now.

Parent's story (dad of a self-harming 15-year-old boy)

I mean, nothing prepares you for this. This isn't what they talk about on the antenatal courses; nor is it something you can punish or take away their smartphone for, so what do you do? I remember his mother telling me that the school had called her after some marks on his body had been spotted by other kids during PE class and those kids had gone to the school counsellor. Fair play to them really. He has been burning himself with a lighter for over a year – a YEAR. How did we not know this?

His mother had told him she needed to wait to talk to me and together we would talk to him. He had been in his room all afternoon since, but with his door ajar as she was afraid he would hurt himself. Honestly, I kind of wished she'd just gone ahead and spoken with him because I didn't know what I could say here. It seemed like such a strange thing to do and I had never heard of self-injury. The first thing I did was get online and look up definitions and information about it. Everything kept coming back to mental health. My son had a mental-health problem and we hadn't known anything about it, while he was living right under our noses. That's when I cried. I'm not much of a crier, but I cried and must have been louder than I thought because he came downstairs and he was crying too. He was trying to say that he was sorry while I was trying to say that I was sorry. I just held him and we cried together for what felt like a long time. I had so many questions, so many things that I wanted to say, but I had no words to articulate any of that. Maybe that's a good thing. Maybe we needed the tears first so the words could follow. That started us down the confusing path of adolescent mental health. We saw the GP, we went on a waiting list, we tried to see a private therapist, but it took us a while to find one who works with teenagers who are actively self-harming. We went to therapy ourselves, and after about six months we all went to family therapy together.

We did get an appointment with state services, and they offered some therapeutic sessions and quarterly reviews with a psychiatrist as long as he was attending his weekly therapy. Medication was prescribed and he took that for the best part of a year and I think it helped. Honestly, I think it was a combination of medication, therapy for him, therapy for us and therapy altogether that got us and, more importantly, him through this. That was two years ago now. He's still in therapy and things are okay, and I'm okay with that too – it's taken me two years to get to a place of feeling that okay is actually okay, but you know what, it really is and I needed to learn that too.

'My journey out of self-harm' (19-year-old female)

The most common thing people ask when they see my scars is 'why did you do it?' It's a strange thing to try to explain. I was carrying a lot of feelings inside myself, but I felt like they were invisible, even to me. No one could 'see' what was wrong with me. But when I could see the cuts, feel the blood, suddenly my pain was visible – it was this cut, this wound and I could take care of it and make the pain feel better. I think that's why I did it. But of course that didn't work because the real pain on the inside was still there and just demanded more and more cuts to reveal itself. Suddenly the cuts didn't bring relief; they were just a symbol of the pain. They became subsumed by the internal struggle and I felt back at square one with it all… now what? I think that's why I got careless about hiding it. I wanted to be caught so that someone else could help me find another way. You can't always speak these things when you're young and still finding the words to express yourself. Asking for help is hard because of this. I needed the help to find me, not the other way around.

It takes support, time, patience, acceptance and empathy for someone to move from self-harming to self-supporting strategies. This is not an easy pattern to break – I want to be clear about that. It has often been going on for a long time before a parent discovers it or a teenager brings it to their parent seeking help. Recovery from self-harming behaviour is a process and it takes time. I feel strongly that you should reach out to your GP and seek a referral to mental-health services, but I also appreciate that we would all want to know what *we* can do around that process to ensure we are supporting our teenagers at home:

- Ensure that you are spending 15 minutes per day one-to-one with your teenager, doing something fun, something that allows you to connect.
- Find ways to slow down, lower your commitments as best you can (for yourself *and* your teenager) and have as much free time and time to relax as you can.
- Encourage your teenager to reach out, talk about this with friends (if they feel comfortable doing this) and to spend time with their friends to connect.
- Take 15 minutes each day for relaxation together (going for a walk, writing a journal, drawing, using a mindfulness app).
- Exercise together (yoga, Pilates, walks, runs, football, cycling, swimming).
- Sit together and create a contact list of safe and trusted people that your teenager can reach out to call or text when they are feeling overwhelmed.
- Make a similar list for yourself as you will need people you can reach out to as well.
- Accept how your teenager is feeling in any moment and empathise with their emotional struggle.
- Be patient, be tolerant, be calm – it takes time to break this cycle.
- Communicate with your school to ensure that your teenager has appropriate emotional support while they are in school.

Professional support is important but those of us in this field who provide that support also know only too well the importance of supportive home and school environments. Strong and supportive parent–teenager relationships are also vital in ensuring that teenagers can work through these complex emotions and develop healthy strategies to counteract their emotional trigger points.

Teenager's story (16-year-old boy)

What I want my parents to understand is that being a teenager is hard. Teenagers are their own people and our opinions aren't worth any less just because we're young. Our mental health is really important and shouldn't be dismissed and brushed aside because they might think that I'm too young to even have mental-health issues. This is something that I think lots of parents get wrong about their teenagers' lives. They think that if we get angry for a genuine reason, like something we have good reason to be angry about, that we're just being moody and hormonal. That drives me mad; it makes me feel like I don't have a right to feel angry about something or that my anger isn't real because I happen to be a teenager feeling that way. I might be arguing with you for a really good reason, and when you dismiss my feelings as 'hormones' it's like you're telling me that my feelings don't matter and that I shouldn't bring them to you.

EATING DISORDERS

I have worked extensively in this area over the span of my psychotherapy career and the impact an eating disorder can have on the parent–teen relationship is a devastating one. Eating disorders are not exclusively an adolescent phenomenon; indeed I have worked with children as young as nine years old with a diagnosis of an eating disorder and also with adults well into middle age. That said, eating disorders do disproportionately affect teenagers or start in adolescence. Eating disorders are also not exclusively a female experience; I have worked with a number of adolescent boys and young men who are living with this diagnosis too. However, it is disproportionately a female disorder. Why this is the case is less clear, with the exact root or cause of an eating disorder being unknown, though we do look at particular variables that might contribute to this mental illness.

- **The biology:** If a teenager has an immediate relative (i.e. a parent, sibling) who has had an eating disorder, they are more vulnerable to developing one themselves due to a genetic link.
- **Emotional disturbance:** If your teenager already has a diagnosis of anxiety or depression they are more susceptible to developing an eating disorder.
- **Environmental/Sociological:** There is an emphasis on thinness being the ideal body type in western culture and this permeates the fashion industry and is perpetuated by the media.
- **Competitive sports:** If your teenager is actively involved in a hobby/sport that values or even requires a lean body type or a light body weight this can also play a contributory role here. Examples of this include gymnastics, ballet, swimming, athletics and horse riding.

George's story (17 years old)

George was 17 years old and training to be a jockey when he was referred to me for psychotherapy. He had completed an eating disorder in-patient treatment programme and was transitioning back to his 'real life' as he called it. Spending almost six months in hospital is quite something to transition out of.

He said that he was 'mortified' that he had an eating disorder and that it had taken him months to be able to even accept that to himself. He said that he thought it was a thing that only girls developed (another myth propelled by the media).

George was a competitive horse racer and had been training to be a jockey for what felt like his whole life. He had been a short and slight kid and had shown early promise in this area so had been taken on by prominent trainers in that industry to nurture and develop his natural talent. He said that once puberty started, his body changed and he suddenly had to work harder to maintain the right body weight and shape. He was terrified that after all these years training that he would 'fall at the final furlong' as he said.

He was very clear about how his eating disorder started – a need to manage his body shape, size and weight. He spoke about how his parents and trainers encouraged and supported him in this endeavour. He said he was holding a simmering anxiety that he wouldn't make it as a professional jockey and would let down all of these people who had worked so hard to get him here. He was able to link this 'out-of-control' feeling with the 'very in-control' feeling his food restricting gave him. This is how he started to restrict more and more. Initially the weight loss worked for him and he was praised by his parents and trainers for his commitment and efforts. But then it stopped working for him and he spoke of losing that in-control feeling. He no longer felt that he was controlling his food or body but that it was controlling him and the anxiety that this was defending against suddenly rose up and overwhelmed him. So he responded by restricting more and more and he became weaker and slower rather than stronger and faster, as he had wanted.

It all came crashing down with a tumble. He passed out while riding his horse and was very lucky to escape serious injury as he fell under the horse mid-gallop. He was admitted to hospital and transferred to the psychiatric wing where he entered their eating-disorder programme. He spoke of having to relinquish all *control while he was in there and how difficult that was and how his struggle to let go of control definitely delayed his progress for the first couple of months of the programme. But he got there and now was looking at what his life looked and felt like when not struggling with control all of the time. Our work was on this point and on exploring who he was outside horse racing, a sense of self that had not yet emerged in his adolescent development.*

Control is central to adolescent development. It is a phase of development that is loaded with a desire and need to pull away from parents and authority figures, experiment with new tastes, experiences and friends, discover who they are and become independent people. It's also a dance of control, wanting control, needing control, taking control, being overwhelmed by control, seeking to control the control. Your teenager needs your help with this, and that doesn't mean that they need you to come in and take over that control but to stay with them while they develop an emotional mastery over the control impulse.

We live in a society that places immense emotional charge on not what the body can do but on what it looks like. Thinness has always been enshrined as a body ideal, and yes the body positivity movement online is making inroads towards changing or at the very least challenging this false ideal, but we have a very long way to go on it. In my work with teenagers who experience eating disorders or eating-disordered thinking (troublesome and intrusive thoughts that negatively impact them and their lives even if they physically haven't developed an eating disorder), I frequently hear the word 'fat' used as a feeling. *How are you feeling today? I feel fat!*

When I explore this statement further, what I see time and again is that feeling fat has become a type of code language for feeling emotionally insecure, anxious, avoidant, rejected and unimportant. With eating disorders (and I include eating-disordered thinking in here), the body is speaking to the teenager's overwhelming struggle to secure a sense of self, a sense of acceptance of the self and a sense of emotional safety/security. It is as though achieving a particular body shape/size/weight is the only way they believe that they can gain mastery over these basic needs for safety, acceptance and emotional stability. Rituals, beliefs and fantasies about food and an idealised body type become the sanctuary they turn to when they feel they cannot turn to somebody else to provide this basic need for emotional nurturance for them. And this so-called ideal body is not just the size-zero model for girls; our teenage boys are also being bombarded by a body ideal, one that is a rather regressed cultural ideal of a strong, tough, macho male who is physically buff, has a six-pack and is, you guessed it, *perfectly in control.* Teen TV shows, exposure to pornography and the social-media-filtered life through a lens all uphold these ideals and contribute to what can become a manic and out-of-control pursuit of perfection for adolescents.

So how do you parent through and around this? What can you practically do? Starting as early as you can, try to implement these:

- **Encourage healthy eating habits in your family:** Speak about how food is there to fuel our bodies so that we can be energetic and active and enjoy life. Talk openly about how our bodies cue us to eat when we are hungry and to stop eating when we are full. Make time for family mealtimes and emphasise that food is a social activity too. Sit around the meal table and talk, laugh, share and connect over the food you are eating.

- **Lead by positive example:** Take time to examine your own attitudes to food, eating and your body. How do you speak about your body in front of your children? How do you speak about food in front of your children? Avoid terms like 'clean eating' as it infers that some food is dirty in comparison. Avoid incentivising your children's behaviour with food: *You can have a chocolate bar if you finish your homework* or *Don't feel sad; let's get some ice cream and you'll feel better.* Do not use diet language around your children. This would mean not counting calories/points/unit/syns or anything like this in front of them – do not reduce food to numbers. Allow your children to see you eat healthily and that includes occasional 'treat' foods while not overtly labelling them as such. Allow your children to see you be active and enjoy exercise as something you choose to do rather than have to do. Do not pat so-called problem areas of your body, or pull at your tummy flesh, because they are watching you. Give them something to absorb that will build healthy body image, and let them hear you say *I love my body. I love all that it allows me to do.* Do not use body-based nicknames for your children *Stretch, Pudge, Buddha-Belly, Tubs, Skinny Malinky* or indeed any nicknames that are about how they look.
- **Critically discuss media representations:** Sit with the magazines or scroll through social media together. Make it a game to spot the edits to an image, what filters have been applied, how much Photoshop has been used. Critically assess what is real and not real. Play with those apps that allow you to edit an image to perceived perfection. Teach your teens how to interpret the obvious but also the more subtle and hidden messages behind the media messaging they are bombarded with. Talk openly about body prejudice and how to identify and challenge it when they see it.

- **Parent with esteem:** This means using your respect and admiration of your child (intentionally seeing the good) to actively invest in your teenager's self-esteem though ideally not starting this process in adolescence but rather strengthening it at a time when they really need their self-esteem cups topped up. Self-esteem is not achieved with body talk. Pay attention when your teenager speaks – physically turn towards them and look at them when they speak. Praise their efforts regardless of the outcomes of those efforts. Let them know that they are smart, engaging, funny and loveable, exactly as they are.

If you do suspect that your teenager has an eating disorder or is developing eating-disordered thinking (more common that you might think), step in quickly.

- Talk about the dangers of excessive dieting or emotional eating – it might be helpful to source an article or video that you can read or discuss together as a reference point for your conversation to avoid personalising it too much.
- Talk to them in a loving and accepting way while being honest about your concerns about weight change, restrictive eating or overeating.
- Make an appointment with the doctor together for a medical check-up.
- Consult with a specialist dietician and/or mental-health professional on this and do so as early as you can. Treatment for an eating disorder will often be a combination of individual psychotherapy sessions for your teenager, parent psycho-education sessions for you, dyadic and/or family therapy sessions.

15-MINUTE SELF-ESTEEM ACTIVITIES

Building and supporting self-esteem and expanding self-efficacy, which is a secure sense of *look at all I can do* remains extremely important throughout adolescence. Your teenager will naturally seek and then demand increasing levels of independence at this stage of development, and they do need this, but they also need you, their parent, as a sort of cheerleader communicating that they are capable of what they want and need to do. You can tell them how great and capable they are, but always remember that to be effective in impacting self-esteem, your praise must be specific and focused on their effort over the outcome.

- Sit facing each other and tell each other five things you love about the other person (usually easy).
- Now tell each other five things that you love about yourself (often not so easy) – do not jump in and rescue your teenager if they struggle here but hold the silence with a smile and sustained eye contact. After a minute of silence, say something like, *It can be hard to think about yourself in this way. Would you like to borrow one of mine about you to start with?*
- Repeat back what you each say about each other and yourselves, for example, *So you love my smile, my baking, the way I sing and dance in the kitchen, that I can speak up for myself and those I care about, and that we enjoy the same TV shows* (based on the list your teen says about you, and have them repeat back what they heard you say about them). Then repeat back to them what they say about themselves too: *You love your extra ear piercing,*

*your dyed hair, how jogging in the rain makes you
feel, your eyes and that you are a great friend to
others.* This way you are amplifying what is said to
ensure it is truly heard.

You can also structure this into a worksheet-style questionnaire,
but I like to write questions on slips of paper and place them
in a bowl or jar and we take turns to pull one out and answer
it. You can add these onto Jenga blocks as part of feelings
Jenga or take large dice and paint over them so that you can
write on them or simply stick these statements onto the dice
with glue. These are the questions and be prepared to honestly
answer them of yourself too. You can answer these of yourself
but then switch and answer them about each other too:

- My friends think I'm great because...
- My teachers say I'm great at...
- I feel very happy when I...
- Something that I'm really proud of is...
- I make my family happy when I...
- Something special about me is...

You can build a self-esteem jar for your teenager. What I
really like about this is that it is not time sensitive and you can
start it as early as you like and keep contributing to it so that
you can gift it to them on their 18th or 21st birthday or simply
keep it accessible so that at a glance they see how much
good and positivity you see in them or can dip into it when
they need to top up their own love cup as they negotiate
through their adolescence.

- Take a mason jar (make it an optimistically large one
  for this) and keep a stack of coloured notelets.

- Write down what you love and admire about your child – these should be character traits, actions, who they are. Write down the actions your child takes that make you so proud of who they are. These can be big, stand-out things or small, everyday things. In reality a blend of the two is ideal.
- You will find that you fill your jar with things like (and this list is intended to give you some structure but you do not need to follow it and it is not exhaustive so feel free to add your own. In fact please do so):
  - I like who you are because...
  - You're really good at...
  - You feel good about your...
  - Your friends think you have an awesome...
  - Somewhere you feel happy is...
  - You mean a lot to...
  - Others think that you have a great...
  - I think you're really good at...
  - Something you really enjoy is...
  - You are proud of yourself for.../I am proud of you for...
  - Your future goals are...
  - I know you can achieve them because you're...
  - You are naturally gifted at...
  - Others often praise your...

In addition to the **self-esteem jar**, you can encourage your teenager to practise *esteem-based reflection* each day. I find that this works best if you do one for yourself and sit together to fill it out if they struggle to do it. You can suggest a journal, which is nice as they can flick back over it on more difficult days or, again, they can simply write on coloured notelets and place these into a jar as a visual reminder. Use some statement prompts to structure this (and you can assign a colour to each one if they are doing it as a jar):

- Something I was great at today…
- Today it was interesting when…
- I made someone smile when…/I smiled when someone did/said…

Challenge play is a great way of building self-esteem and expanding self-efficacy.

Balancing activities: This one is called **beanbag balance.** Have your teenager see how many beanbags (the small square ones – you can buy them or quite easily make them) your teenager can balance on their heads while walking a distance (e.g. to the other side of the room), turning around and walking back.

An alternative version to this one is **cushion balance**. Have your teenager lie on the ground and raise their legs. Balance one cushion on their feet and have them hold and wait for your signal before they kick the cushion as far across the room as they can. Repeat with two cushions, then three and maybe even four, so that you are raising the level of challenge in line with what they can gain mastery over.

Balloon balance: This is a fun game to play with teenagers as well. You can do this one in a number of ways so that you can play with just the two of you or add in others for some group or family play. Hold an inflated balloon between you and your teenager (between tummies, shoulders, elbows, hips, etc.) and move across the room keeping it in place without touching it with your hands.

Make it a **balloon relay** by having two teams (i.e. at least four people) each work together to move across the room, holding the balloon between their shoulders, then turn around and get back to the start before the other team do. An added challenge here is to have more than four people so that each pair has to pass the balloon to the next pair (or just sub in an additional person) without touching the balloon with their hands.

Play **over/under** as a family. Stand in a line behind each other, facing each other's backs. The first person (let that be you to start) passes a balloon over their head and the next person passes it behind them under their legs; the following person passes it back over their heads and so on so that the balloon is passed over, then under to the back of the line (family). Then turn around and pass it back the same way. On a special occasion when you have a house full of people, split into two teams and race each other doing this, but when it is just the family, time yourselves and see how quickly you can do this without messing up the sequence.

Staying on this theme of using challenge play to stay connected, here are some activities that you probably played in some way when your teenager was younger. You might be surprised to find they still appeal and work now.

Straight-face challenge: This is when you look at each other and take turns being the straight face. The straight-face person has to maintain an absolutely straight face while the other person tries to make them laugh either by gently touching (there is a no tickling rule and no touching more sensitive areas) or by telling jokes or pulling funny faces. Then swap over roles and repeat.

Thumb, arm or leg wrestling: You might know the thumb- and arm-wrestling techniques but are perhaps not so familiar with the leg wrestling one. So to play leg wrestling you both lie down on the ground, side by side but facing opposite directions, and link arms. This means your hip is at approximately the level of the other person's shoulder. Your legs are lying flat on the ground. To begin, you each lift your inside leg up in the air (toe tap if you can but it's not necessary) three times. After the third time, you lock legs and the goal is to flip the other person over. You can find a video of this activity by searching leg wrestling on YouTube if a visual would make this description easier to understand. This is an adaptation to the more traditional thumb- or arm-wrestling and is more suitable to older children and teens. It is a great one for parents to play with teens as you might be similar height and build and they may be more likely to engage in this one because it is more complex with increased challenge than the other variations. The other variations are also fun to play at this age.

Wheelbarrow walk: You may not have done this one with them since they were kids but suggest it in a playful way that wonders, or even dares, to see if you can still do it now at this age. They lie face down and while you lift and hold their legs by the ankles, they walk across the room on their hands. This can be tiring on their arms so it is best in short bursts. I like to structure it a bit by placing something on the floor that they have to walk towards, then around and back again. I have also facilitated this one while adding in some nurture by having a box as the target object but placing a sweet on top of the box so that they have to bend and pick up the sweet with their mouth before turning and coming back. There is a good level of touch, but it is touch that is a logical part of the activity, and the pressure of walking on their arms provides good proprioceptive muscular input so it is also really regulating while being fun.

Speaking of nurture, our teenagers still have high nurture needs but may find it harder to ask for or even accept nurture from us. Sensory and nurture play is very effective in achieving emotional regulation. So we have to find playful ways to offer and invite nurture and sensory play into our connections with our teenagers. **Pretzel/Donut** is a feeding game. Place a pretzel or a mini-ring donut or even something like one of those iced party-ring biscuits that have the hole in the middle, on your index finger. Now invite your teenager to see how many bites they can take before biting through the ring. I've had a 15-year-old take ten bites before the pretzel snapped off my finger.

ALCOHOL AND DRUGS

It probably isn't a great surprise to learn that young people (adolescents into mid-twenties) are the group most associated with irresponsible drinking. Our focus should not solely be on the issue of underage drinking but on the broader problem of excessive drinking or binge drinking, which is drinking with the intent of getting extremely drunk. Our teenagers are growing up in a culture of problematic alcohol consumption. It is quite normal to *prink*, which is pre-drinking or drinking at home or in someone's home before you go out to drink, and means you will save money on the cost of drinking in a bar, but if you are underage it also just means that you will get drunk faster when you meet up with your peers.

I asked a friend of mine who has parented two teenagers up to the late stages of adolescence now what her stand-out learning was from parenting teenagers and what advice she would give. Without hesitation she replied:

*Get them involved in sport or scouts or music or something like that as early as possible. This gives them a sense of identity and belonging so that they're less likely to stray into drugs or alcohol. Let them know early that drinking alcohol under 18 is illegal and that you **will not** allow it in the house or elsewhere. Come down hard on this before it's an issue so that they're clear about your stance on this; be very clear that you will* not *tolerate it. Explain the effects of drugs and alcohol on young developing brains. Tell them stories of people you know who are addicts and the impact that it has had on their lives, and if you don't know anyone, find a TED talk that deals with this and watch it together.*

My friend felt that this boundary was of vital importance in parenting teenagers and she believed that making a really big deal of it before it was an issue both ensured that her young teenagers knew where she stood on it and instilled a pause impulse in them when they were faced with a choice around drugs and alcohol with their peers. The research out there backs this up. A widely reported study[14] of 5700 teenagers aged 13–14 years old and 15–16 years old in schools in England found 'young people are more likely to drink, to drink frequently and to drink to excess if they … are exposed to a close family member, especially a parent, drinking or getting drunk'. The research tells us that encouraging and developing strategies that involve the adolescent's most dominant social influencers – parents, teachers and peers – effect a meaningful and sustained change in perceptions and behaviour.

Education and moreover parent-led education is the answer to instilling personal responsibility. In order to make an informed choice on how to drink in a responsible manner, people must be educated from a young age about the consequences of drinking irresponsibly. This makes teachers and parents the most important influencers in teenagers' lives on this issue. Further, for this to be most effective, young people need to receive targeted education on the risks associated with excess drinking *before* they even consider consuming alcohol socially, that is before they get to establish cultural norms and behaviours around drinking to excess. So you need to be having this conversation early and often if you want yours to be the message that they default to when the choice presents itself – and it will present itself.

You may not be able to stop your child trying alcohol or drugs, but you can be the benchmark of safe habits around alcohol and stress caution about drug use. You are the greatest influence your child will have on these topics so you need to go back to your risk audit (as detailed in Chapter 3). In addition, reflect on your own relationship to alcohol and/or drugs and think about some of these questions:

- Does your child/teenager see you drinking alcohol at home/ out in public?
- Does your child/teenager ever see you drunk at home/out in public?
- Has your child/teenager ever been woken by you coming home drunk after a night out? Did you discuss this with them the next day?
- Has your child/teenager observed you with a hangover? What is your hangover routine (staying in bed, not getting dressed, vomiting, ordering takeout, lying on the sofa)?
- Have you ever had to cry-off from taking your child/ teenager to their weekend sporting activities because you had a hangover?
- How old were you when you first tried alcohol/drugs? What was that experience like for you? Do you regret it?

- What is your attitude to young people drinking? Do you think they should not use alcohol/drugs underage at all? Would you suggest that they try it at home with you the first time? Do you turn a blind eye to your teenager taking alcohol to a party at their friend's house or their friends doing so in your house? Would you buy alcohol for your teenager?
- What is your attitude towards drugs? Do you think some drugs matter more than others (e.g. no to a class A drug but more relaxed about them using marijuana for example)?
- What is your level of knowledge and understanding about various drugs and the laws around drugs?

When I deliver my parenting teenagers psycho-education events, I am invariably told by someone that they do not know anything about drugs or the drug scene among adolescents.

Parents' story about their teenager experimenting with drugs

After one of these events, two parents hung back to the very end when even all of the other parents who had hung back with more private or sensitive questions than they felt comfortable asking in the group had left. They were hesitant and apologised before they started. I reflected that they seemed unsure and uncomfortable and wondered what I could do to help. They described their youngest son, a teenage boy of 16 years old. They spoke about him adoringly and lit up as they did so. He was such a lovely boy, kind and hard-working. He helped around the house and had never given them a moment's concern or worry... until a few days earlier.

They described how he had been hypervigilant for the post every day during the mid-term break. When they had asked him about this he had said that he was waiting for a delivery that was a surprise gift for Father's Day (which was coming up), and because that would be just like him, they accepted it and turned a blind eye to it. However, the delivery had arrived after the mid-term break had ended and his mother had signed for it at the door. She noticed that it was very small and flat and didn't look professionally packaged like something you might order online. The stamp at the top showed it came from Holland.

His mother said she couldn't explain it but it just didn't feel right and she had opened the package. She said she knew this was wrong and an invasion, but as he had said it was for his dad, she didn't think it would matter that she saw it. What she had opened was, in fact drugs, which her teenage son had ordered online from overseas and had delivered to her home. She had taken a photo of what was inside and looked up images online until she found one that matched. From this she learned that these were class A drugs. Another internet search highlighted how dangerous this was, in terms of personal risk, but also how illegal it was.

She couldn't believe it and didn't know what to do. So she had done nothing at all for a couple of days but set about informing herself about the drugs in question and the potential consequences for what he had done. Then she told his dad, who had taken a different approach and marched straight into his son's room demanding to know what he had done, how he had done it and how long he had been using drugs. Neither was prepared for his response. He told them it was no big deal, everyone was doing it, they were out of touch and then he challenged them on having opened his post.

They were floored. Why wasn't he embarrassed and contrite? Was this normal? Were they out of touch?

We spoke about the legal consequences for importing class A drugs into the country and how it could just as easily have been the police at the door with the package as the delivery person. We spoke about boundaries and limit-setting, something they hadn't ever really addressed head-on with this son as he had never openly pushed boundaries or challenged them. We wondered if his casual response meant this was his first time doing this or first time taking drugs like this. We planned for the conversation they needed to have with their son and moreover I suggested we took some time together around this conversation as they had to process their son not being who they thought he was and explore what this realisation meant for their relationship. Discovering that your teenager can do something that is so far removed from anything you had ever considered them capable of and is something absolutely against your own family moral standards is very difficult to process.

I directed them towards a youth organisation that could support them and their son through this issue with drug use and could offer a drugs education programme for all of them, and they decided themselves to have a lawyer relation of theirs sit with him and talk him through the legal consequences for importing class A drugs and the penalties for this. I helped them to work on relearning their son and seeing all sides to him. Their years of idealising him as their 'easy child', 'the good one', openly telling everyone that 'he never gives a moment's worry' or 'oh we're not worried about this one; he would never let us down' had blindsided them to his need to individuate and to do so by establishing that he was not who they were, or who they wanted him to be. Yes, he had taken this to an extreme but were there signs that he wasn't 'perfect' all along (who is after all and, moreover, who wants to be? As the famous child psychoanalyst Donald Winnicott said, 'Perfection isn't good enough – good enough is good enough'). Why hadn't they seen that? Why hadn't that been good enough. This was a relationship redefining moment for all of them, and with work they did emerge better connected from this experience.

I share this story for a few reasons. One is to highlight that there isn't a 'type of kid' who gets involved in drugs. Another is to reflect that drugs are pervasive in our culture and therefore this is something as parents that you have to address with your children along with the alcohol conversation. And yet another reason is to gently yet firmly challenge you to question your view of your child now that they are a teenager. This does not mean to do so negatively but to take time to see them with fresh eyes and perspective.

15-MINUTE EXERCISE

- Describe your teenager as though you were doing so to someone who has never met them before.
- Now consider your teenager through someone else's eyes. How would their friends describe them among themselves?
- Think of someone you know to be critical of your teenager, perhaps a peer, a relative, a teacher, coach, and describe your teenager as that person would describe them.
- Summarise this into three positive qualities that your teenager has and two more challenging qualities they have.

- Reflect on whether this has changed your view of your teenager. This means how you see them, not how you feel about them. Have you learned something new from this reflection? Maybe you have seen something you didn't want to or maybe you are seeing them in a more positive light and this reminds you not to always look at what they are getting wrong.

Part of parenting a teenager is, as I said at the start of this book, to grow your parenting up as they grow up. This includes seeing them in all of their parts. Their good, of course, but also when and how they will make poor choices – and they *will* make poor choices. Ensure that you remove your *not-my-child blinkers* and allow them to show you their successes and their struggles because that is how you stay connected through adolescence. It is about communicating that *I see, accept and love all of you* and about using your emotional connection to convey *together we will get through this*.

Something else that stands out for me in this case study is that defence claim of *everybody is doing it*, the *all of my friends are allowed to – why can't I* type of defence. We talk about pester power in early and especially middle childhood but this *everybody else* defence is closely aligned with that one in terms of it being designed to wear you down and get you to give in to the demand. And, often, it is quite effective. But it brings to mind the influence of peers in our teenager's behaviours and thought formation. It is hugely significant across the board and particularly so in this area.

Many studies point to peers (and also parents) being the most significant predictors on individual behaviour.[15] I talked about peer influence in Chapter 6, but it is also very relevant here. For lots of teenagers, trying alcohol is a part of their assertion that they are not children anymore. They see this as a way of mirroring adult behaviour, but also trying or ongoing consumption of alcohol can be an attempt to fit in or be accepted by their peer group. Often teenagers enjoy the way alcohol makes them feel in terms of being less inhibited and less self-conscious. Or some might like alcohol because it gives them a sense of excitement that forbidden behaviour brings, or perhaps it is that it makes them feel that they're more of a 'grown-up'. A key developmental task of adolescence is to become increasingly independent and to learn how to make responsible decisions and choices that they can take responsibility for, regardless of the outcomes. It stands to reason that some of these decisions will be good and some will be downright poor decisions, and this is okay and to be expected because making mistakes and learning from them is all part of growing up.

However, alcohol consumption affects teenagers' ability to think quickly, make good judgements and identify, and therefore avoid, dangerous situations or negative risk-taking behaviour. For most young people, there won't be long-lasting damage from mild alcohol experimentation, but for others the consequences are long-term and far-reaching. For this reason, we must take alcohol consumption in adolescence very seriously. In addition, because their bodies are still physically developing and they may not know or be able to predict their tolerance levels or the impact alcohol can have on them physically, they will need to have this explained to them as part of this parent-led education.

Alcohol has a variety of effects on the adolescent body and may not even affect them in the same way each time. As adults, we know that initially you might experience feeling energised, social, engaged, relaxed and fun while drinking alcohol. And it is important that we are honest with our teenagers about this, as if we only speak about the negative signs and they try it and feel the positives, they will have cause to distrust what we tell them. So acknowledge that they might start out feeling good, but as they drink more or as the alcohol has more time to enter the bloodstream, they will experience more negative effects. These might include poor coordination, becoming clumsy, slurring of speech and the capacity to think/act slowing down. If they keep drinking beyond this point, they may even start to vomit, become sleepy or even pass out. They may find that they can't think clearly or act in accordance with what they are thinking or picking up from the people around them, or that the environment they are in leaves them vulnerable to accidents, violence or even death if they were to lose consciousness, stop breathing or vomit while unconscious.

It is important to reflect these as facts rather than fear prompts (though they may well be scary) and to reflect that if everyone around them is also drunk, they will not be able to see what is happening or take action to save them; nor would they be able to save a friend.

The same applies to experimenting with drugs and potentially worse. I worked with an adolescent aged 17 years old in a psychiatric setting. He had tried MDMA (also known as ecstasy/molly and is a synthetic drug chemically similar to both a stimulant and hallucinogenic) just once. He had suffered a strong brain chemistry reaction and it triggered a psychotic break from which he did not recover. He was a long-term in-patient who was catatonic (in an immobile and unresponsive stupor) most days and was not going to recover from the effects of the drug on his brain. The risk with taking drugs is that we do not know what we are predisposed to and what the mind-altering chemical we are ingesting might trigger in the brain. Further, we cannot ever really know the quality of the drug in question, what it may be cut and mixed with and what effects that combination could have on our mind or body.

And don't just assume that your teenager gets these risk factors associated with drinking or trying drugs. Bear in mind that they are neurologically wired to engage in impulsive, reward- and thrill-seeking risk-taking behaviour while the part of the brain that enables them to identify and weigh up pros and cons is not yet developed. They cannot adequately assess the level of risk in terms of potential outcomes for their actions because they are governed by a more exciting part of their still-developing brain, and for this reason they rely on the education, input and advice of parents. They might not thank you for it because, let's face it, *thanks for those boundaries and limits you set for me* has been said by no young person ever, but they will thank you for it in terms of how they live and grow and continue to make choices and decisions that affect their life and the lives of those around them.

DELINQUENCY

Delinquency is improper, criminal and illegal behaviour enacted by a teenager. It is a broad definition, and the struggle can be that some of what falls into this category seems mild and almost normal. Stealing is one of the most common examples of delinquent behaviour and is something at which *many* teenagers will try their hand at some point. This is not to excuse it; stealing is a concerning behaviour and should be treated as such. But there is a difference between a teenager shoplifting and a teenager who holds up and robs a shop. Essentially, delinquent behaviour is behaviour that does not conform to the legal or moral standards of society. It usually applies only to acts that, if performed by an adult, would be termed criminal but as a teenager would be more likely to see you cautioned, placed on a diversion programme and, if a pattern of such behaviour exists or a significant escalation occurs, subject to juvenile justice up to and including youth detention centres.

Sociologist Howard Becker[16] referred to four types of delinquencies:

1. Individual delinquency (this is where only one individual, who is self-motivated to do this, is involved in committing the act).
2. Group-supported delinquency (these are those acts that are committed while in the company of others who are already engaged in such activity).
3. Organised delinquency (committed by formally organised groups such as gangs/criminal organisations).
4. Situational delinquency (less discussed in literature but, unlike the other forms, the causes are not seen as deep-rooted but the assumption is that means and motives for delinquency are often relatively simple, with the perpetrator showing poor impulse control and usually feeling they have little to lose if caught. It is more spontaneous and opportunistic than the others).

STEALING AND ENTITLEMENT IN ADOLESCENCE

Stealing can be the behaviour that really throws a parent. I've had countless parents exasperated that their teenager would shoplift from a large department store when they have everything they need or even want given to them. Sometimes, this is where the problem lies. Perhaps your teenager is stealing from *a sense of entitlement*. Perhaps they simply want something that someone else has and, without a second thought, they take money from your wallet to get it. Might this be because they have always been handed what they want/need without understanding that money is worked for and the desired items are saved for? Have they had opportunity to contribute as a member of your family? Have they had to perform unpaid chores because being part of a family means that everyone helps out? Have they had opportunities to undertake additional chores and responsibilities to earn pocket money so that they can save for something that they want? Have they ever tried to get a job (babysitting, cutting grass, cleaning, etc.) and is this something that you have actively encouraged in them?

Keep in mind that developmentally your teenager believes they have left that age of command (do as you are told) and have entered an age of consent (I'll do it if I want to or if it suits me to do so), and with the ongoing egocentrism of development, *because I want* is a powerful motivational force that underpins behaviour. This will make even more sense when you remind yourself of how their brain is developing with the pleasure-seeking and reward drives calling the behavioural shots. Think about it this way:

- 'When I want something, I want it a lot.' This places increased importance on my desires.
- 'If I want it a lot, I must have it.' This brings in a sense of urgency and it is no longer something I simply want but quickly becomes something I need.
- 'If I need it, I should have it.' This is the entitlement.
- 'If I don't get what I believe I am entitled to, it's unfair.' This brings me to a self-righteous stance whereby if I am denied the thing I want and feel entitled to have, I am being deprived of my right to have it and I will feel a grave injustice has occurred against me.

In this stance of entitlement and feeling as though I have been wronged in being denied what I want, I may well feel entitled to simply take it without too much thought before or afterwards. After all, I want/need/am entitled to/being denied my right to 'it'. Why wouldn't I take it? It's what I should have. And in this headspace, when you ask me, *Why did you steal that?* I am likely to blankly stare at you while I shrug and say, *Because* you *wouldn't get it for me; this is* your *fault because if you had got it for me I wouldn't have had to steal it.*

They are not sad or disappointed that they cannot have the thing they want; they are angry and even full-on furious at the denial. As parents, you have to be able to withstand this irrational fury and hold a boundary in place, set a limit on behaviour and uphold consequences for behavioural transgressions with someone who will still believe that they were in the right and you were in the wrong. It is hard to do so-called 'positive parenting' in the face of this negative and often thankless stand-off.

Adolescent entitlement exists in smaller, more everyday situations too. In fact, adolescent entitlement is often the bugbear of the unappreciated parent! Maybe you know what it is like to give and give and always be thinking ahead to anticipate their needs before they even get to know that they had that need. And yet, they don't thank you, don't acknowledge your efforts (your shortcomings yes, but not your efforts) and you end up feeling frustrated, irritable and snapping at them in what they feel is an unjustified and unreasonable manner because they may not automatically see that your actions on their behalf warrant overt declarations of appreciation, believing moreover that it is 'your job' to meet their needs/demands/wants because you are their parent.

And, maddeningly, they really believe it when they say this to you. I find that this is often one of the most challenging aspects of parenting teenagers that comes up time and again: *they never appreciate me or what I do for them*, and from the teenager's point of view: *they have to do this for me – they're my parents; it's their job!* I hear it so often that I wonder if it is about something other than appreciation.

If you take the teenager's response and really hear it, try speaking it aloud a number of times. Might it say more about not feeling that they are worthy of all you do for them, not feeling deserving of your efforts and attention so it is easier to minimise it as something you *have* to do rather than something you *choose* to do for them? Acknowledging it as something you choose to do for them means having to accept that you feel they are special and deserving of your efforts and that is only possible if they have the self-esteem to integrate that they are someone deserving of those efforts. That is not easy for an adolescent, and part of the challenge of parenting through entitlement is reflecting that you are not entitled to all of this but you are deserving of it. This is parenting with self-esteem and parenting towards self-esteem.

15-MINUTE ACTIVITY FOR SELF-ESTEEM

Safe-place pillow: I have used this activity in my work in domestic-violence shelters and children's homes and it is one that I feel can also apply here when we are talking about playful routes to building self-esteem.

You are going to decorate a pillowcase with phrases, words, statements and pictures using fabric markers. These should be things like words, positive affirmations, positive memories, reassuring self-talk statements and coping skills. The purpose is (and explain this clearly to your teenager) to create something to sleep on that is a reminder of how great they are, how strong, how resilient, deserving of good things, so that they feel safe, calm and confident about themselves last thing at night and first thing in the morning.

I have used this with young people who experience anxious sleep and/or nightmares and middle-of-the-night waking.

With bad dreams, I use the movie/director technique (see the second book in my 15-Minute Parenting series), so I suggest they draw a positive change to the dream onto the pillow and sleep on it. But even just using the positive statements and words will be very reassuring should they wake in the middle of the night from a bad dream.

Supplies needed:

- White or pale unpatterned *pillowcases*. Buy cheap ones rather than taking one from a set you have at home.
- *A large piece of cardboard* to put inside the pillowcase so that what is written on one side doesn't leak on to the other side.
- *Fabric markers:* You will need fabric markers and some of those require you to iron the item after use to ensure they don't transfer, rub or blur. For this reason, I tend to go with the Sharpie Stained Fabric Markers as they are straightforward, have thin nibs for writing messages clearly and do not need to be ironed afterwards.

Tips: Consider making one for yourself too because this can be something really nice for you to have. You can make it a more reciprocal activity by having your child design one for you and you do one for them, or consider co-working on each other's so that you each write positive statements about yourselves as well as each other.

It is no coincidence that a section that started with defining delinquency quickly tracks to a piece on self-esteem. Self-esteem is an antidote to delinquency and also a deterrent because it is easier to build it gradually over time than play catch-up when someone is already engaged in delinquent behaviour.

Stealing can occur as a result of that sense of entitlement, but this is not the only reason a young person will steal. Other reasons a young person might steal include but are not limited to the following:

- A feeling of not being loved or not fitting in (at home/with peers). Hurt people tend to hurt people and if a teenager is hurting inside, they may well act out in a way like this to lash out at those they don't feel are there for them. Start with emotional reassurance – this does not mean ignoring or excusing the behaviour but explaining it and conveying that you still love and accept them when cross or disappointed with their behaviour.
- Feeling unseen, unheard or overlooked in the family. If a teenager feels like this, a behaviour such as stealing is a good way to get them front and centre of your attention. Always remember that what can seem like a demand for attention is often a need for connection. Correct this behaviour within a loving and secure connection. To this end, it might be useful to listen attentively to the emotions behind what they are saying and discuss their feelings in a positive non-judgemental way.
- Wanting to pay for or simply steal something to give as a gift to friends/family in an attempt to fit in/be accepted.
- Perhaps the group they are trying to get in with engage in shoplifting and they want to be accepted so they do the same.
- Stealing money to fund the purchase of drugs or alcohol. This may not be limited to money – your teenager might also steal jewellery, electrical items, phones and so on.

- A misplaced desire for independence whereby they want to be able to buy what they want, when they want by themselves.
- A more basic desire to have what others have.
- A sign of bullying in terms of them being bullied to hand over money to someone else.

So what do you do when you discover something like stealing?

- **Be certain:** When you discover something is missing, pause and look at the situation from every angle, considering every possibility before you jump to a conclusion. If you are about to accuse your teenager (or indeed anybody) of stealing, be certain before you act.
- **Invite self-confession:** Before you challenge, reflect aloud that something is missing and it is something you want returned so you will be looking into where it has gone. Mention that if it was taken in error it can be returned without trouble and it can all be talked about calmly.
- **Accept:** Whatever your teenager tells you in terms of where they got money, start by accepting their story and reflecting that you understand what they are saying but because it doesn't make complete sense to you, you will be checking with whoever was named as source of item/money in the next two hours. This gives them time to come and correct the story themselves rather than you having to go full Sherlock Holmes on them. Self-correcting behaviour should always be encouraged.

Serious behaviours warrant serious discussion

- Name the behaviour as serious and that you are taking it seriously.

- Ask them to name in as much detail exactly what happened in sequence –before the event, during the event and immediately after and then a while later. Include reference to how they were thinking and feeling at each stage. Take your time with this step as you really want them to recall what happened in terms of the action they took but moreover how that action was underpinned by thoughts and feelings each step of the way. Ask them what they would do differently looking back, and why. Ask them how it has felt to talk about this with you. Reassure them that you love them but will not tolerate this behaviour going forward.

Then say, 'Now I will tell you this story but from my perspective…'

- Start by condemning the behaviour in the clearest terms: stealing is wrong and no matter what you think, there is always a victim. Emphasise that stealing is an illegal act, a crime, and the potential consequences include a criminal record and a day in court and/or probation services so that the impact of a quick act can last a lifetime. Be very clear about future consequences and the steps you will take and who you will involve. In saying this, do not predict that their future is a criminal one in prison. Be realistic yet hopeful. That is something you will work with them to avoid and this is why you are taking it so seriously because you know their future is bright, positive and hopeful and want to keep it that way.
- Talk about how it is part of your role as a parent to teach and uphold morals, rules and boundaries and that you take this role really seriously. Clarify that this is the first time it has happened and because it is you want to address it directly with them at home *but* if it were to happen again, you will involve anyone else you deem relevant, such as police, store management, school. Talk about how you

believe in them, you believe that they know better and can do better and you also believe that anyone can make a mistake and this is why you are taking the approach you are.

- Talk about social reputation – theirs primarily – and how this could get them a name/reputation for such behaviour, but also talk about your own social reputation and that of your family. Your teenager is part of a system bigger than themselves; that system is your family and they have a duty to uphold and live in a way that is respectful of others in the family. Their behaviour reflects on all of you.

- If the compulsion to steal is active and has been present for some time then it may well have or could become a habit, and habits are hard to break. Consider that you will need to reach out beyond your family to a psychotherapist for support to address this compulsion.

- Talk about desire and fulfilment. The truth is that it is okay to want things, to desire nice things, but that doesn't mean that we get to have everything we want. No one gets to just have the things that they want. Things have to be worked for, saved for, earned. Proactively find ways to instil this with structuring pocket money into what they can spend, what they must save, what they must donate, and ensure that this is adhered to.

- Share how you feel about this, emphasising that it doesn't change how you feel about them, that your love is constant and unconditional but that you are hurt, let down, shocked, incredulous, sad, upset, disrespected, devastated (be authentic, don't just throw words at them, stick with how you truly feel).

- Tell them what it feels like not to be able to fully trust your own child. Explain that this trust has to be repaired between you and that you are prepared to work towards that and you wonder if they are too. Talk about how trust is the basis of all relationships; it is the glue of connection and yours has been ruptured, and while it will repair, it will take time to get there. Explain that for a while you might need to question and then check if what they have told you is true; you may feel some emotional distance or coolness between you, but this is because you are feeling upset about what happened and you know it will pass in time. Let them know that you think this reflects on you as much as them and has left you questioning how you parent, that you feel guilt and even shame that you didn't do right by them. Explain that you don't want to be the parent who searches rooms, bags, coat pockets or phones and ask that they do their part so that you don't have to become that parent. Ask them what they would do or say if they were the parent here – don't accept a shrug, wait for an actual answer to this.

- Your core message is that you love them no matter what and your core direction is that they must never steal again.
- Enforce payback (in addition to and not in lieu of other consequences). Sit and make a plan for how they will pay back *all* of the money that was stolen or replace the item that was stolen *in addition to* the other consequences and the need to repair the trust in your relationship.

Consequences are really a parental choice so I tend to avoid anything that might seem as though I am prescribing those for you. That said, perhaps keep the following in mind as you do come up with consequences:

- **It should fit the crime:** Borrowing something without permission is not the same as stealing from your wallet, and the consequence should reflect this. Similarly, the risks involved in stealing outside home versus inside home should also be reflected (that is not to say one is not a bad behaviour; both are, but potential fallout from one is higher than the other).

- **Be creative:** If you are restricting social activity and freedom (i.e. grounding or taking phone/social media away, etc.) add in that they should volunteer with a local organisation or charity or should commit to five to ten hours' volunteering a week for a month. They could undertake to complete a charity run that they train and raise money for and promote the cause. These more pro-social and creative consequences will also form a sense of being a valuable member of their community, which is good for self-esteem and is really helpful to dissuade them from doing this behaviour again.

- **Promote honesty but avoid shaming:** Tell them that you won't lie on their behalf if someone asks you why they are in trouble, but you will not shame them. This means that you will say that they did something that crossed a big line and that they are in trouble because of it and it will take some time to fix this. You will not tell people that they stole because that is their truth to tell, not yours, and you will support them if they do want to be open and honest with others about what has happened.

- **Be fair:** Once they have acknowledged and accepted their part in what happened and worked to repair the ruptured trust and followed your consequences for the behaviour, you have to let it go. You cannot keep whipping it out like a figurative stick to beat them with every time they don't do something: *You didn't empty the dishwasher like I asked you to. This is just like that time you stole. I cannot trust you.* For repair to be authentic it has to be embraced by both of you. If you find that you cannot let this go and are remaining hypervigilant of your teenager and their behaviour in spite of the above, consider consulting with a psychotherapist yourself to help you better process what has happened and how you continue to experience it.

Mutuality and trust are key to a connected, secure relationship. Mutuality is based on the premise that a healthy connected relationship is one that is rooted in mutual giving and respect. A healthy relationship is two-way. There must be give and take on both sides to make it work. A one-way relationship would be one based solely on what the individual (i.e. your teenager) wants and demands for themselves with little regard to others in that relationship. A mutual relationship is based on reciprocity: *I will do my part and you must do your part*; consideration: *I am sensitive to your needs and ask that you be sensitive to my needs/needs of others too'* and compromise: *No one gets everything they want all of the time. Let's find a way to meet somewhere in the middle on this one.* The egocentrist nature of adolescent development drives home the importance of instilling an appreciation for moderation in how we parent our teenagers. That is about controlling their need for instant gratification with delay: *You can't have it now; you must work towards having it;* and denial: *You can't have what you want.* Integrating the value of moderation, especially as it relates to impulse control and better management of the desire for gratification, is about emphasising that relational harmony/contentment is more important than the gratification of every desire. This is the very essence of *good enough is good enough*, which has been my parenting mantra throughout these books.

15-MINUTE EXERCISE: RESTORATIVE REFLECTION

You can either list these as bullet points or make it more of a visual/graphic style of flow chart. Include these questions that your teenager must answer alone and ensure you give them time and space to do so.

- What happened? They must provide a summary but as much detail as they can here.
- What was I thinking at the time? They must reflect on their motivations and beliefs in the moment.
- What have I thought about since? With some time and space how has my thinking about my actions changed?
- Who was affected by my actions and how? This is towards the restorative piece whereby they must think about all actions having consequences for themselves and others.
- How can I make things better? They must think about making repair and moving forward.

Mutuality, trust, moderation and connection are the building blocks to parent through adolescent entitlement too. But it is not easy to uphold this as a parent because our teenagers do not thank us for these limits, though they really need them. Entitlement is not all negative and in balance can be evidence of confidence, self-esteem and an ability to assert what we deserve and are due. We want our teenagers to feel entitled to safety and respect in their peer relationships and interactions. This is a pro-social benefit of entitlement. But balance is the key word and it is parenting with those pillars of mutuality, moderation, trust and within connection that hold the sway of that balance and keep us all in check emotionally and behaviourally.

CHAPTER 9

The Next Chapter of Parenting

At this stage, you might well be aghast. *What, another chapter? When does this end?* The truth is, parenting never ends. It grows, it develops, it adapts, it changes but 'it' is a constant. This next chapter of parenting is that transition from adolescence into (young) adulthood.

I always think the journey or trajectory of parenting can be summed up through the eyes of our children. In the early years (0–7 years old) they are utterly besotted with us, we can do no wrong and are the source of all knowledge in their lives. In those middle childhood years (8–12 years old) they are becoming more cynical in the way they view and think of us. They see we have limitations and believe that we need to be held to account for these limitations – by them. In adolescence (13–18 years old) they are intensely disappointed in us and are not afraid to show us that disappointment. We are embarrassing, clueless, unreasonable and unfair in their eyes. And in young adulthood (19–25 years old) they are beginning to see that they may have been a little harsh in how they judged and assessed our parental performance and there is a more overt attempt at relational repair and connecting at a more mature and adult level than before. You know that you have reached adulthood when you can recognise that your parents have limitations and you love them anyway.

And so this chapter of your parenting journey marks the end of adolescence but not the end of parenting. I find a reassuring sense of contentment in that. I hope that you do too.

BEING A PARENT OF AN ADULT CHILD AND BEING THE ADULT CHILD OF AN OLDER PARENT

Tolerance is the key to this stage of parenting. If you are privileged enough to still have your own parents in your life, take time now to reflect on what and how it feels to be the adult child of older parents.

- What words come to mind to describe the nature of your relationship as an adult with your older parents?
- What feelings come to mind?
- How do you experience your parents now? What is their role in your life and are you content with that?
- How do you imagine your older parents experience you as an adult child in their lives? Are you content with this?
- If you could change anything about your parenting journey (with each of your children), what would that one thing be? This can be as intense or light-hearted as feels right for you. I like to invite parents to do this reflection as it applies to each of your children to give each relationship its due attention but also to highlight how your parenting journey with each of your children has been different, both for you and for them.
- If you could change anything about your own child–parent relationship with your parents, what would that thing be and why? Is there time or scope to change this now?

Focusing on tolerance is to mitigate the simmering impatience and frustration that adult children can feel towards their parents as, gradually, the roles start to shift with a parent eventually relying on their adult child to support them to varying degrees. As parents of young children we focused on fitting our children into our adult lives, and as parents of adult children the task is to ensure we still fit into their lives. As they continue into adulthood and start relationships, careers and families of their own, that 15 minutes of connection a day may well become 15 minutes a week as they have new and more demanding priorities than us parents. If this is your truth, start a tradition of sending a text/message every day without need for a response just to communicate *you are always with me*. And if what you get is 15 minutes of face-to-face time per week, make that work for you. Plan a walk, to sit together in the garden, share coffee and a cake for your 15-minute distraction-free connection time each week. If your adult child has had cause/desire to relocate too far away for regular in-person time, build it into the technology and coordinate a coffee and cake connection via a video call for 15 minutes a week. The job in parenting is to raise independent adults. That doesn't mean there isn't a painful adjustment to what your adult-child living independently actually means to you. And perhaps this is the role you have relished and counted down to, meaning more freedom and independence of your own without the daily demands of parenting. This is absolutely valid and worth enjoying. The relationship evolves but the connection sustains. Your adult child will still need you and their relationship with you. They will still seek and need your connection, mindful attention, interest and approval. You are always your child's champion and emotional support, regardless of age (yours or theirs).

You need to plan for transitioning from parenting your adolescent to parenting a young adult, to parenting a fully grown adult.

The **young adult** part of this transition can be a tricky one and you will have some wins and some losses along the way. Learn from both and commit to integrating that learning so that you might both do better as you move forward. Communication and connection are key. You have to step back and afford plenty of space and opportunity for your young adult to do things for themselves while remaining emotionally available for those moments when increased self-reliance brings some serious errors in judgement along the way.

For me, this stage of parenting a young adult comes back to boundaries and communication. And yes, I started this book about parenting adolescents using the same phrase. The structure doesn't change greatly across the span of parenting. The language doesn't change but the tone does and must change in order to stay effective.

If your young-adult child is living in your home, the boundary remains that this is *my home, my rules*. This doesn't mean you necessarily hold them to a curfew of your choosing *but* it might well mean that you say they cannot bring intimate partners back to your home without prior discussion/agreement. It is okay to want to know whom you might bump into on your landing. It is also okay to expect a working young- adult to contribute financially to the running of your home in terms of food, bills and so on. You may choose to hold that money as a form of saving for when they move out (so that they can move out) or you may want/need to use that money. Either is fine. It is okay to share your thoughts and opinions, and more than that I think it is really important that you do so because even if they roll their eyes and dismiss what you've said, your words echo inside while they make those choices and decisions. Be open, be available and know how and when to be hands on and hands off.

It is challenging to feel that you have lost that role of being the centre of your child's life and are being pushed closer to the sidelines. Bear in mind that it can also be difficult for your young-adult child to realise that their needs are no longer the centre of your world either. This is a push/pull relationship with a difference. This time you are gently yet firmly pushing them closer to independence and full autonomy while being available to pull them in when they crash and burn and need their emotional love cups topped up again (yes that continues to be a need throughout our lives).

The ideals you hold are, likely, quite different and more modern than the ones your parents upheld. The ideals that your young-adult children subscribe to will also be different in their bid to do it their way – the more modern way. This disparity of ideals is a significant gear change in your parenting connection with them, as you may feel misaligned in your world views/approaches to life and also be faced with having little to no say in that disparity because your child is 'now an adult' and responsible for their own choices and decisions.

The way to emotionally connect through this disparity is to go back to agreeing versus accepting. Acceptance is key as you prepare to negotiate this disparity. Remember, as already discussed in this book, *acceptance does not equal agreement*. Your two opposing views can emerge and co-exist without it interrupting your connection if you embrace this point. Accepting the limitations and failings of our parents yet loving them regardless is crucial to assuming an adult existence. Take time to reflect on the areas of disparity between how you and your parents view the world. Perhaps some of those have lessened as you have aged too but regardless it should show you that what frustrates you and your young-adult child now is not that dissimilar.

LETTERS FROM PARENTS AT VARIOUS STAGES OF PARENTING FROM ADOLESCENCE TO ADULT CHILDREN

I asked parents to share with me their experiences of parenting through adolescence and here are some of the reflections that were shared with me to include in this book.

A parent whose eldest child is just entering adolescence

The thing that I'm most looking forward to in this phase of parenting is to see the people they will grow to become, to witness their chosen journeys and to have fun conversations with them as they do all of that. But the thing that scares me most about parenting in this stage is the awareness I have that something outside our [parents'] control could happen to them! Something that we can't protect them from once they start to separate more from us. That's scary as a parent for sure. Looking back on my own adolescence, I wish that my own parents had understood that I wasn't an extension of them and their image, as I sometimes felt I was. I wish they knew that my emotional sensitivity wasn't a weakness or character flaw but was actually a strength that has stood me in good stead as I have grown in my own parenting now. It took me years to really recognise my sensitivity as a strength because of this. And if I could go back and whisper into the ear of my adolescent self I would say, 'I'm worthy to be in any room and good enough is good enough. What other people think of me is not within my control; nor is it even about me.'

A parent of teenagers

I find it exciting to watch my teens explore what the world has to offer them, and I see it as my role to support them on their quest to be what/ who they will become and to encourage them to follow their passions. My goal throughout this phase of parenting has been and continues to be teaching them to respect themselves, their health and bodies and also to be respectful of others. While I want to give my teens the freedom to explore, I have to acknowledge what frightens me the most is the peer pressure to engage in risky/dangerous behaviour such as drinking alcohol, experimenting with drugs and unsafe sex. Behaving a certain way to fit in with their peers is of course what typical teenagers do, but I want them to be brave enough to be themselves and do the right thing regardless of popular opinion. And I want to help them to be able to navigate these issues for themselves without being stifling.

Something I wish my own parents had known when I was a teenager was that sometimes teenagers are confused and make stupid decisions and that this is okay. It's better to discuss what's happened with them and to try to help them become more confident in their decision-making than to be impatient or dismissive with them and their behaviour.

If I could go back and whisper into the ear of my teenage self I would say, 'You don't have to conform. It's okay to be yourself and to follow your own path so please don't feel restricted by the opinion of others, especially as they may not have your best interests at heart. It's okay to fail and try something else.'

A parent of a child on the cusp of adolescence

I have been taking stock of the lessons we have all learned from those middle-childhood years and now, as I start to look forward to what might lie ahead for us in our parent–teenager relationship, I find that I am most excited about growing up the conversations we have always shared with her increasing depth of understanding emerging in those conversations. I look forward to maturing our shared love of reading and movies and discussing what we read together too. I am really looking forward to being able to go out of the house for a walk on my own or with my partner and being able to leave the girls alone knowing that they can take care of themselves and each other.

I find that I'm fearful of social media and its role in their lives. It's not something I engage in and am challenged to start engaging with it so that I might better support the girls through it. Peer pressures, sexualisation (of girls in particular), what dating will look like, issues of domestic violence, sexual assault/rape, consent, alcohol, drugs are all present in my mind. Above all of this though, I am most fearful that we may lose the connection and openness that we've established and that they may start thinking that they're invincible and know it all without reference to us, the way that teenagers do. This is, in part, what I would whisper into my own teenage ear if I could. I would say, 'Things are not as black and white as they seem.'

15-MINUTE ACTIVITY

Take 15 minutes and ask/answer the following questions:

- What excites you most about the prospect of parenting teenagers?
- What frightens you most about the prospect of parenting teenagers?
- What is one thing that you wish your own parents had understood when you were a teenager?
- What is one thing that you wish that you had understood when you were a teenager? What would you whisper into your own teenage ear if you could?

I also asked an older parent, now parenting grown adult children and grandparenting their children for her reflections on all of this too. Here is what she says.

I was asked a question of my experiences of raising adolescents. This set me thinking and my thoughts first went back to myself and to my own upbringing. I was quite a strong-minded adolescent. I recall feeling strongly that if I was old enough at 16 to get a job then surely I was old enough to make my own decisions. On reflection, my parents were very subtle in how they got me to do their bidding in spite of this.

Roll on the years and there I was faced with the task of dealing with my own adolescents. The girls were the stronger willed and would stand and argue, sometimes to the point of exhaustion, on both of our parts I think. Honestly, I found it frustrating that they were now independent young women trying to make their way in the world. The boys seemed easier at that stage, in part because they didn't argue in nearly the same way. I think now it was largely because they never really listened and just did their own thing anyway.

As I look back now, I believe that I misinterpreted some aspects of adolescence insofar as I believed that it was a case of the girls taking on their mothers and not their fathers, and the boys just being allowed to develop. When I look back on that I can say that my belief in this regard has evolved and changed – perhaps too late for parenting my own teenagers but not too late for parenting my adult children or in how I grandparent my teenage grandchildren, especially when they bemoan their mothers to me.

Today I observe my teenage grandchildren and how they react to their mothers and I've got to say, I don't think that much has changed. They talk to their parents in much the same way as my children did to me. The difference now is that it's all played out on social-media platforms and body image/social perception and opinions of their peers matter more than your parents'. This was always a feature of parenting teenagers, but I observe that the role of social media is to amplify this a lot louder and a lot faster than when I was parenting teenagers. I'm so grateful I was parenting my teenagers before social media was a factor.

Would I change anything if I were back at the beginning again with my children? Maybe. I think now that perhaps I was as much a problem for them to deal with as I thought they were for me. Being totally honest about it, I was afraid to let them grow and make their own mistakes because I felt that I would be made redundant in their lives. While I'm grateful I parented before social media, I do wish I had access to more of the kind of parenting books that would have allowed me to explore ways to acknowledge and address those anxieties when we all reached this stage of parenting through adolescence.

Have you ever heard of the *sandwich generation*? This is people who are adult children of older parents while also parenting adult children of their own. I spoke with one such parent to get her take on the lessons to be gleaned from being of the sandwich generation, and this is what she told me.

What is the best thing about being an adult child of a parent while also being the parent of an adult child?
My mother has always been a strong and positive influence on my life and I am very thankful that my girls, all of whom are now adults, have had so much time with her in their lives. My own grandmothers were both dead before I hit eight years of age so my memories of them are very hazy. My girls will carry forward their very clear memories of their grandmother and indeed will be able to pass on her stories to their children in time.

I think that this particular time in history is also very interesting from a female perspective. My mother was a young mother during the second wave of feminism (in the 1970s) and so my girls have a great insight into the path that women's equality has taken – how far we've come and how far we still have to go. Finally, I love that my daughters have played a really strong part in helping my mother (now 85) in understanding the kinds of issues that we have lived through and even voted on in the last decade. So, the intergenerational education has been a two-way street.

What is the most challenging thing about this?
The most challenging thing about having an elderly parent who needs quite a lot of support in order to continue to live at home, while also having young adults at home, is having to decide on priorities. I struggled with this for a while. Whose needs come first? At times, I felt that I was being pulled in all directions. It was horribly stressful until I had a moment of clarity when I realised that I had to decide

on priorities, much as I didn't want to. It's like triaging patients in the emergency room.

So, my kids had to come first always, followed by my husband and my grandchildren. And then my elderly parent. Now that I have that clear in my head it makes life much easier. It's also something that I've felt was important to communicate to my siblings. We have to put our own families first. And elderly parents can be very demanding and often insist on things being urgently attended to when they aren't urgent at all. This prioritising has given us all clarity. Tough love, I guess.

What surprised you when transitioning from parenting adolescents to parenting young adults and a grown adult?

My daughter got married a few years ago and at her wedding she paid tribute to the fact that I gave her the freedom to be herself and to follow her own path. I was surprised at this, because she is my eldest and like a lot of parents I would guess, I felt that she was very much the guinea pig for my parenting. I often felt that I hadn't a clue where I was at, particularly during her teenage years. I muddled through and I know I made some awful mistakes. So, to know that she felt she had the freedom to be who she wanted to be was very surprising and gratifying.

Once your kids reach 18 or thereabouts, I do feel that a lot of the active parenting has to stop and that's easier said than done. I think you have to change from actively setting boundaries and rules to an advisory role (except for rules of the house – they stay). But if your child wants, for example, to quit college and go to work, I think you have to support that even if it's not perhaps what you had in mind.

I generally give advice when asked for it. But otherwise I just let them know that I'm always in their corner, even if the path they're choosing is not necessarily what I think is right for them. Because you know what? Parents aren't always right.

I believe if you've given them a strong foundation, if they know you're always there for them in a non-judgemental way, they will find their way. The most important thing now that they're adults is that they can come to me and talk to me about whatever messes they've made, whatever problems they have and I'll listen and do everything I can to help. But I can no longer walk ahead of them, sweeping away potential pitfalls and crises.

The hardest lesson of parenting is to learn to let go. You move from being their guide and their teacher to their support system, their safe place, their home in every sense of the word.

I am so grateful for the parents who spoke with me to share their lived learning from their parenting journeys.

PLAY IS FOR LIFE

And now I want to talk about keeping play alive through this transition. Play is for life. Play equips adults to be more creative and flexible thinkers. Being playful is a key way to get more out of life, and while it is an essential component of childhood, it remains essential in adulthood too. Young children learn skills to be able to work in groups, share, negotiate and resolve conflicts but those same skills remain a key aspect of (young and full) adulthood too. A capacity to play and be playful helps to complete us all as more emotionally well-rounded and joyful adults. Play allows us the opportunity to pause and unwind. Simply watching children at play is and of itself often enough to spark joy that lowers tension levels in our minds and bodies.

I wrote of being playful within your intimate relationship in the first book in this series (play without an intimate agenda that is), but the same principles are relevant here. There are many research papers into this topic and one such study[17] found that more playful young adults (i.e. those who self-rated with high levels of spontaneity or described themselves as energetic and as enjoying fooling around) tended to report less stress in their lives and displayed better coping skills.

Embracing a playful state of mind and way of being is good for your brain and body as you grow and develop. It keeps you young, engaged, energetic, enthusiastic, curious, imaginative and connected with others and the world around you. Play for teenagers and young adults is a great way of modelling that *fitting in* should never be at a cost of their mental health and well-being. They should not feel that they have to dull their edges to be accepted, and treating play as a core component of your relationship with your children, regardless of their age, is a great way to model this as a way of being.

Sing: Out loud and often, and it doesn't have to be good, no matter what your young adult, masquerading as Simon Cowell, tells you about that.

Have yourself a daily silent disco: Put on your headphones, play music of your choice that only you can hear and dance like no one is watching – even if they are. If you can do this and allow your young adult to see you with creative, fun-filled, carefree abandon you will spark joy in them and give them permission and an invitation to also embrace playfulness. They may or may not join you in the singing and dancing; it doesn't matter as simply bearing witness to *your playfulness* will be an opportunity for shared joy.

Trying new things: This is a form of playful risk-taking. Again, this can be something you do with your young adult or simply ensure they see/observe you doing. This could be a life-drawing class, a calligraphy class (maybe even a dirty word ceramic painting class – there is a class for everything – as it is fun and a bit cheeky, which increases its playfulness), a yoga class with a difference (voga, anyone?), a pottery class (very sensory), a dance class, sea swimming, taking up the ukulele and joining a local musical group – or anything else you've wondered about and not taken up before because the demands of life didn't allow it.

Smile and seek opportunities for laughter: Smile often, at people in the street or shops, with the people in your life wherever you can. Practise laughter, share jokes, share funny stories of things that happened or something you heard about.

Tell stories: Life is full of stories. They are everywhere when you start looking for them. Share your stories and ask your young-adult child to share and to keep sharing theirs with you.

Spend time with children in your life: Observing children at play, joining them in their play when possible and appropriate is a great way to stay playful in yourself.

Curiosity: This enables playfulness. Be curious about people, life, new experiences. Go to new places to do new things so that you meet new people outside your more typical peer group.

Suggest fun things to do together: Suggest things to do together and be open to rotating between your choice of activity and theirs. Be open-minded and give everything a go.

Take a game from childhood and play it now: I know this sounds far-fetched and I fully acknowledge that play is a key part of my professional life and the talks/seminars/training events that I do (be warned if you ever come to something I am speaking at in any capacity, you will be invited to play) so it may seem as if it would be easy for me to suggest this but honestly, *try it* and if it is abhorrent, don't do it again...

but I know it won't be. I have played everything from The Hokey-Cokey, Head, Shoulders, Knees and Toes (including a snazzy jazz version a colleague taught me) to Duck, Duck, Goose with adults and with parent–teenager (older) groups. When you embrace and invite play, anything is possible and fun is guaranteed. If I am losing you here, start a step back and play charades or Pictionary at your next family gathering.

Parenting is about connection and play fuels connection. Make time for fun and to play in your life and particularly in your ever-evolving role in the lives of your young people.

A LETTER FROM JOANNA

I want to say a huge thank you for choosing to read my 15-Minute Parenting series. If you did enjoy it and want to keep up to date with all my latest releases, just sign up at the following link. Your email address will never be shared and you can unsubscribe at any time.

www.thread-books.com/joanna-fortune

Why 15 minutes? is the most common question I get asked about this book series and my answer is this: in my clinical practice with families, the most common thing I heard from time-poor parents is that after finishing work, negotiating traffic, doing the childcare pick-up and getting home to get a dinner on the table they feel lucky if they have 15 minutes with their children before it is bedtime. I heard it often enough to embrace that 15-minute window and develop therapeutic, play-based parenting strategies that will make that 15 minutes work for you and your child in a way that will lead to *fewer tears and more laughter*.

In the teenage and young-adult years it becomes less about negotiating traffic but about finding ways to stay relevant in the lives of our young people, and aiming to secure a 15-minute connection each day becomes the optimum. A consistent and predictable moment-of-meeting each day will always be transformative in your parenting connection with your children, regardless of their age. Parents often baulk at the idea of playing with teenagers, thinking it makes sense with the young children but teenagers don't like to play, do they? Yes. Yes, they do. But you have to make play possible. Make play inviting. Make play appealing. So you have to find ways to grow up your parenting while remaining playful to sustain that all-important connection. I hope that what I have written here has inspired you in that regard.

As your children grow and develop, securing that 15-minute window to mindfully connect with them each day will prove more and more valuable – and *even the busiest teenager can give their parents 15 minutes a day*, right?

Parenting is not an exact science, and there are so many differ-ent and even conflicting schools of thought out there that getting it right or even mostly right most of the time can seem like an impossible goal. And just as you have it nailed, your children only go and grow up a stage so that what was working before no longer seems to. We need strategies that contain the flexibility to carry us through our children's various developmental stages; in other words, we need strategies that help us to grow up our parenting as our children grow and develop, and this is why there are three books in my series, to carry you all the way from the *cradle to the rave.*

In this third book in my series, I really wanted to spotlight the possibility and moreover the transformative power of play in the parent–teenager relationship, because I believe play and playful connection to be very important, yet under-discussed aspects of adolescent development.

What I wanted to create here, and hope that I have done so, is a road map to ensure that playful connection between you and your adolescent can be sustained throughout this time of intense physiological, neurological and psychological change.

I hope you loved my 15-Minute Parenting series and if you did I would be very grateful if you could write a review. I'd love to hear what you think, and it makes such a difference helping new readers to discover one of my books for the first time.

I love hearing from my readers – follow me on my Amazon author page or get in touch on my Facebook page, through Twitter, Goodreads or my website.

Thanks and remember... play is a state of mind and a way of being, regardless of age, so make time for play!

Joanna

JoannaFortuneSolamhClinic

@TheJoannaFortun

www.solamh.com

@joannafortune

Joanna Fortune

NOTES

1. Dr Stephen Porges developed a theory around the social
   engagement system (SES) as part of his polyvagal theory. In
   the parent–child relationship, an available and supportive
   parent co-regulates a young child as they meet with and
   master challenging experiences so that not only the very
   physical presence of that person (parent) is calming for that
   child as they grow but their psychological presence (because
   we hold important people in our minds even when they
   are not physically present) continues to soothe, calm and
   reassure us in stressful situations.

2. Dr Ed Tronick of Harvard's Child Development Unit has
   researched the impact of emotional rupture and repair in
   healthy parent–child relationships as part of his 'still face'
   experiments.

3. Brooks, D. (2019) 'Students Learn from People they Love',
   New York Times, 17 January.

4. Dikker, S. et al (2017). 'Brain-to-Brain Synchrony Tracks
   Real-World Dynamic Group Interactions in the Classroom',
   Current Biology. 27.10.1016/j.cub.2017.04.002.

5. Marsh, P. et al (2006) 'The changing nature of adolescent
   friendships longitudinal links with early adolescent ego

development', *The Journal of Early Adolescence*, 26(40) pp. 414–31.

6. Peter Fonagy and Anthony Bateman are founders of the therapeutic modality mentalisation-based treatment (MBT).

7. I talk about this further in my TEDx talk *Social Media – The Ultimate Shame Game?* TEDx Dublin 2017, www.youtube. com/watch?v=ORhwrL71dYc.

8. Dahlgreen W. (2015) '1 in 2 young people say they are not 100 per cent heterosexual', YouGov, https://yougov.co.uk/ topics/lifestyle/articles-reports/2015/08/16/half-young-not-heterosexual (accessed 17 August 2020).

9. Video by the National Youth Theatre of Great Britain in 2017 entitled 'Do you know your LGBTQ+ alphabet?' as part of the Join the Conversation movement: http://www. youtube.com/watch?v=x6fLxvKWzak.

10. National Union of Students (2014) *Education beyond the straight and narrow: LGBT students' experiences in higher education*, London: NUS.

11. Konrath, S. H., O'Brien, E. H. and Hsing, C. (2010) 'Changes in dispositional empathy in American college students over time: A meta-analysis', *Journal of Personality and Social Psychology Review*, 15(2) pp. 180–98.

12. Bleakley, A. et al (2008) 'It works both ways: The relationship between exposure to sexual content in the media and adolescent sexual behaviour', *Journal of Media Psychology*, 11(4) pp. 443–61.

13. Centres for Disease Control and Prevention (2018) Morbidity and Mortality Weekly report, 15 June 2018. *Surveillance Summaries, 67(8) Youth Risk Behaviour Surveillance – United States 2017.*

14. Bremner, P. et al. (2011) *Young people, alcohol and influences.* Joseph Rowntree Foundation, https://www.jrf.org.uk/sites/default/files/jrf/migrated/files/young-people-alcohol-full.pdf (accessed 14 September 2020).

15. Scholte, R. H. J. et al (2008) 'Relative risks of adolescent and young adult alcohol use: The role of drinking fathers, mothers, siblings and friends', *Addictive Behaviors*, 33(1) 1–33, http://www.ncbi.nlm.nih.gov/pubmed/17490824 (accessed 14 September 2020).

16. Becker, H. (1966) *Outsiders: Studies in the Sociology of Deviance*, New York: Free Press (pp. 226–38).

17. Magnusen, C. D. and Barnett, L. (2013) 'The playful advantage: How playfulness enhances coping with stress', *Journal of Leisure Sciences*, 35(2) pp. 129–44.

APPENDIX A

Stages of Developmental Play

The three stages of developmental play (that typically take 0–7 years to fully develop) are what ultimately enable our children to develop a capacity for emotional self-regulation while nurturing their emerging sense of who they are and their understanding of themselves, others outside of them and the world around them. This is how they develop a capacity for the social skills and emotional regulation that will later equip them to manage stress, gain mastery over tensions and negotiate misunderstandings.

Stage one is that stage of messy, tactile sensory play including sand, water, bubbles, Play-Doh and music. This play that sees your child more fascinated with the box the toy came in than the toy itself because boxes are all about containment and discovering what is on the inside versus outside. This stage of play is about discovering where 'I' end and the world and others outside me begin.

Stage two is where we see our children deepen their understanding of the world outside them by beginning to take in and consider the perspectives of others. They play with little dolls (small-world type play) and have them talk to and interact with each other. Being able to consider the perspectives of others is essential to developing empathy, critical thinking, reciprocity and general civility.

Stage three play is role play but be careful to see this as dramatic play rather than dressing-up play. This type of play is where the play decides what the prop is – for example, a scarf is never just a scarf: it is a magic carpet, a picnic blanket, a bandage, a blanket for a baby or a cape for a superhero – rather than the prop deciding what the play is, such as wearing a princess dress that makes me that princess and nothing else. In stage three play, our children push boundaries and test out what it would be like if they were in other roles in their lives, be that playing at being a parent or a doctor, a teacher, a musician or a builder.

Made in the USA
Monee, IL
03 October 2022

15122361R00166